The Last Voyage of the
Gloucester

Norfolk's Royal Shipwreck, 1682

Edited by Ruth Battersby Tooke, Claire Jowitt,
Benjamin W D Redding, and Francesca Vanke

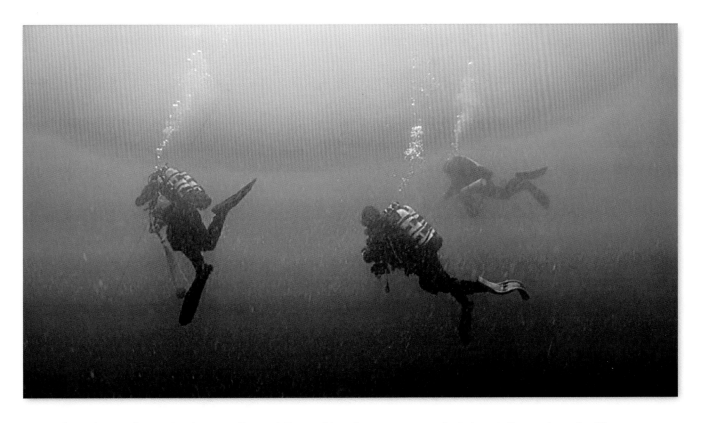

▲ *Back to the surface: the Barnwells and Garry Momber return to their boat. Reproduced with permission of Norfolk Historic Shipwrecks Ltd and the Maritime Archaeology Trust.*

Acknowledgements

This exhibition and its accompanying publication would not have been possible without the advice and assistance of a number of institutions and a great many people over several years. The research underpinning the exhibition was supported by a project grant from the Leverhulme Trust. In addition, particular thanks must go to Lincoln and Julian Barnwell; James 'Tiny' Little; the Ministry of Defence and Navy Command; Norfolk Historic Shipwrecks Ltd; HRH the Duke of Gloucester KG KCVO; General Lord Richard Dannatt GCB, CBE, MC, DL; Henry Cator OBE, DL; National Museum of the Royal Navy; Garry Momber and the team at Maritime Archaeology Trust; Ian Panter and the team at York Archaeology; Geoff Taylor; Richard Endsor; Gwyneth Fitzmaurice; David Kirkham; Ninya Mikhaila; at Norfolk Museums thanks must go to Steve Miller, Jo Warr, Man-Yee Liu and the conservation team; Darren Stevens and the design team; thanks also to the creative team at Eye Film and many colleagues at the University of East Anglia, including David Richardson, Vice Chancellor, Fiona Lettice, Pro Vice Chancellor for Research and Innovation, Sarah Barrow, Pro Vice Chancellor, Arts and Humanities, Matthias Neumann, Caroline Mayers, Simon Dunford, Emily Fairchild, Cat Bartman, Laura Potts, Steve Waters, Mike Bernadin, Chris Blincoe, David Ellis and his team, and current and former drama students who voiced the argument over navigation we feature in the exhibition.

We are also very grateful to our generous sponsors: Adnams plc, Alan Boswell Group, and Birketts LLP.

We would like to thank all our lenders to the exhibition, including The Worshipful Company of Barbers, Blenheim Palace, the Bodleian Libraries, University of Oxford, Museum Boijmans van Beuningen, Rotterdam, The British Library, the Trustees of The British Museum, Doddington Hall, Edinburgh University Musical Instrument Collection, The Fusilier Museum London, Government Art Collection, Lincolnshire Archives, Mount Stuart Trust, The National Museum of the Royal Navy, Portsmouth, Royal Museums Greenwich, Royal Academy of Music, Royal Armouries London, Het Scheepvaartmuseum, Amsterdam, Staffordshire Record Office and Dartmouth Heirloom Trust, and several private collectors. The objects rescued from the *Gloucester* wreck site appear in this exhibition with the kind permission of the Ministry of Defence and Norfolk Historic Shipwrecks Ltd.

Especial thanks go to Alex Gordon-Jones for her tireless efficiency on the exhibition coordination. Without her extraordinary dedication and enthusiasm for supporting every aspect of this complex project, it simply could not have happened.

HRH The Duke of Gloucester KG KCVO

KENSINGTON PALACE
LONDON W8 4PU

Historians find their understanding of historical events by reading contemporary accounts in Journals or letters written by eyewitnesses, or official reports that may or may not be politically biased.

Occasionally insight can be found by archaeological discoveries, such as the identification of the wreck of the Gloucester. The large number of artefacts discovered with the wreckage gives us clues to contemporary naval life and helps us identify both those saved from the disaster and those left behind to drown.

The revelation of the Gloucester reminds us of a particular crisis in our nation's history, when the exclusion issue split politics into Protestants refusing to accept the possibility of having a Catholic King, and loyal Royalists who accepted The Duke of York's legitimacy whatever the consequences.

1682 brought a victory to Charles II and his brother which was reversed a few years later, when William III and Queen Mary replaced James II and his catholic ways and suggested that many people came to feel that as King he was as incapable of steering the Ship of State, as he had proved in May 1682, when the Gloucester sank with much loss of life.

I congratulate those who have put the exhibition together and the Barnwell brothers, whose persistence has provided insight to this significant historic event.

A Word from our Sponsors and Supporters

A great story lies at the heart of most memorable and meaningful communication and the story of the last voyage of the *Gloucester* is no exception. It is a tale that is important and emotional, that through wonderfully preserved artefacts tells us so much about life aboard ship on its final journey, about its principal passenger, the future King James II and VII, his court, and the culture of Stuart society. Adnams is delighted to be able to support the telling of the story of this ill-fated vessel 341 years ago.

In the traditions of great explorers, Julian, Lincoln, and James have discovered for the nation a find of profound historical significance. Only a few years earlier in 1672, the *Gloucester* was also a participant in the Third Anglo-Dutch War at the Battle of Solebay, off the coast of Southwold. Southwold, as our home, sits at the beating heart of Adnams.

The modern day Adnams was founded in 1872. Adnams today is a business proud of its heritage and sense of place, and one that takes its responsibilities to the natural, built, and social environment extremely seriously. The story of the *Gloucester* will become an important part of the social and cultural fabric in our amazing corner of the world, and we therefore felt compelled to work with others to help share perhaps the most important maritime find since the *Mary Rose*. Staging an exhibition of this nature is very much a team effort and I would like to record my sincerest thanks to the teams at the University of East Anglia and Norfolk Museums, and of course to Julian, Lincoln, and James without whom this most wonderful and interesting of stories could not have been told.

Finally, my hope and that of the whole Adnams team is that you enjoy your journey into the world of the *Gloucester* and leave with your own compelling story to tell of a famous British warship that tragically sank on 6 May 1682 on the North Norfolk sandbanks. Enjoy.

Dr Andrew Wood OBE DL, CEO Adnams Plc; Chairman, Visit East of England.

J ulian and Lincoln have been completely committed to this project for twenty years. They have selflessly spent all their spare time, money, and energy on the discovery, all to preserve an important part of our history. I am proud that we have been able to help in our own small way and look forward to seeing their hard work come to fruition in the exhibition.

Alan Boswell, Executive Chairman at Alan Boswell Group.

B irketts is delighted to sponsor Norwich Castle's exhibition 'The Last Voyage of the *Gloucester*: Norfolk's Royal Shipwreck, 1682'. The exhibition tells a compelling story of social and political history and its subject demonstrates how fine margins can change the course of history. The exhibition also spotlights modern day determination, passion, and innovation in revealing how the long-lost wreck was discovered by Julian and Lincoln Barnwell, and James Little. These characteristics are ones that will inspire visitors and sponsors alike.

Chris Coupland, Partner and Head of Agriculture and Estates Team, Birketts.

Contents

Introducing the Finders

The announcement on 10 June 2022 of the discovery of the wreck of the *Gloucester* frigate made headlines around the world. The *Gloucester* sank 341 years ago on 6 May 1682 off the North Norfolk coast while carrying the future King James II and VII (1633-1701). The ship went down with many passengers and crew still on board and resulted in numerous lives being lost. Since running aground on the treacherous sandbanks off Great Yarmouth, the wreck of the warship has lain half-buried on the seabed with its exact whereabouts unknown. Divers Julian and Lincoln Barnwell, along with their late father Michael and retired ex-Royal Navy submariner and diver James 'Tiny' Little, discovered the wreck in 2007 after a four-year and five-thousand nautical mile search.

Due to the age and prestige of the ship, the condition of the wreck, the artefacts already rescued from the seabed, and the political context for the disaster, the finding of the *Gloucester* can legitimately be called the most significant event for British maritime history since the *Mary Rose* was located in 1971 and raised in 1982. To date, approximately four hundred and fifty artefacts have been rescued and conserved. The exhibition 'The Last Voyage of the *Gloucester*: Norfolk's Royal Shipwreck, 1682' explores this internationally significant find and the ship's history. The exhibition is the result of a partnership between the Barnwell brothers, Norfolk Museums Service, and the University of East Anglia. It brings together finds from the wreck site with loans from national collections and private lenders, and shares for the first time ongoing historical, scientific, and archaeological research.

Here we ask the Barnwell brothers, who now run their family business Barnwell Print Ltd, some questions about their lives and story, and the circumstances of their once-in-a-lifetime discovery.

▲ *The team preparing the dive boat Relentless in 2012 before setting out to recover the bell. L-R, Andy, Lincoln, Julian, Bill. Reproduced with permission of Norfolk Historic Shipwrecks Ltd.*

▲ *Julian and Lincoln Barnwell, with a selection of rescued artefacts from the Gloucester, May 2022. Reproduced with permission of the University of East Anglia.*

▲ *James Little's survey vessel the Dornoch, 2005. Reproduced with permission of Norfolk Historic Shipwrecks Ltd.*

Introducing the Finders

▲ *Diving to the Gloucester wreck site, 2018. Reproduced with permission of Norfolk Historic Shipwrecks Ltd and the Maritime Archaeology Trust.*

Meet the Barnwells: Interview with Julian and Lincoln Barnwell

Tell us about what led you to start diving?
Our father Michael Barnwell started diving in 1967 with the East Anglian Branch of the British Sub Aqua Club. As boys we used to watch him dive with his friends and come back with crabs and lobsters. We have fond memories of washing his equipment after a dive. We were both lucky enough to start diving with Dad when Lincoln was eight and Julian was twelve. Together we explored many rivers and mills in the Norfolk Broads. At the age of sixteen, we both qualified with the same dive club as Dad, and soon moved on to diving in the North Sea. A few years later we managed to save up enough to buy our first dive boat together, a 5.3 metre Osprey rigid hull inflatable boat called the *Crusader*.

How are you able to fit diving in alongside running Barnwell Print Ltd?
We would often get up really early to go to work so we could take time off during the day to go diving. We can remember diving before work too. Over the last twenty-five years, we have built up our print business and in 2000 we were able to free up Lincoln's time so that he didn't have to work on the presses anymore. This has given us more time to think about and plan new adventures together and ultimately allowed us to locate the *Gloucester*.

What makes the *Gloucester* shipwreck so important for you? Why did you start looking for this ship in particular?
The *Gloucester* is the ultimate wreck divers' dream. To us it feels a real privilege to bring the ship's story to life and share it with everyone. As the discovery and research on the wreck with our partners on the

project have progressed, we have started to see ourselves as guardians of the wreck site. We feel a real responsibility to all the people on board on that fateful voyage, especially to those who sadly perished at sea.

We have been fortunate to dive many shipwrecks in the North Sea, and in many other locations abroad. We have always enjoyed reading about the history of ships as well as relishing the thrill of trying to locate wreck sites and identifying the vessel in question. Through this reading Lincoln learnt that wooden shipwrecks were particularly interesting, and that these vessels offered different challenges to divers and archaeologists to modern iron wrecks. Back in 2001 Lincoln read Richard Larn and Bridget Larns' monumental *Shipwreck Index of the British Isles: The East Coast of England* and, while working his way through the pages relating to the coast of Norfolk, he found the name '*Gloucester*'. The brief overview in the book of the loss of the frigate included the magical word '*cannon*'. Combined with the fact that James, Duke of York and Albany, was on board, this was enough for Lincoln to phone Julian and say: 'You're not going to believe this: there is an incredible wreck we need to find, but we're going to need a bigger boat!'. This was the start of our amazing adventure, which has become central to our and our families' lives.

Tell us about how you went about finding the *Gloucester* wreck, and when were you sure it was definitely the *Gloucester*?

Finding shipwrecks is easier these days because the majority have been surveyed and are marked on modern charts. Most dive boats are now equipped with digital charts, echo sounders which show the seabed, and side scan sonars which increase the search area to both sides of the boat. For our search for the *Gloucester*, we purchased an offshore coded twelve-metre boat called the *Penetrator*. We equipped it with a magnetometer and soon learnt how to survey the seabed using its specialised software to measure magnetic fields and pick up the deviation caused by ferrous material such as iron cannon and anchors. After finding several eighteenth and nineteenth-century wrecks, in June 2007 we finally had the perfect magnetometer reading. Lincoln and our good friend Andy were the first to dive the site and they knew straight away that we had found an historically important wreck. In 2012, we located the ship's bell, which has the date 1681 on it, a key piece of evidence used to identify the wreck as the *Gloucester* with certainty.

How did you feel when you found it, being the only people who knew about it?

The excitement on the seabed is hard to explain. Not only did we experience the thrill of diving and not knowing what we would see, but when we found such an old wreck site with cannon scattered all over it which might be the *Gloucester,* it was an overwhelming feeling.

Lincoln said 'I soon thought of those who had lost their lives at the time of the sinking. After spending some time kneeling on the seabed with my hands on my head, taking in the moment, I calmed the adrenaline and remembered how I wanted to tell the team on the surface what we had found, but first I had to survey the site. I have often compared this moment to what it must feel like to land on another planet. Then, on the return journey back to Lowestoft Harbour, I felt a sense of huge responsibility but was eager for the unknown journey ahead. This did not alter the fantastic feeling of discovery which we are happy that we were able to share with our late father'.

Your story is especially engaging because of your close relationship. What does it mean for you to have achieved this together as brothers and how has it changed your lives?

As brothers we have always been remarkably close. From an early age we would spend a lot of time together playing and exploring our local area. Our first real adventure was in June 1990 when we water-skied the English Channel. The early morning crossing was completed by Julian, then twenty-three years old, in seventy-five minutes. Lincoln, who was just nineteen, made the same trip in sixty-four minutes! This was a particularly special moment for us as a family because we raised money and awareness for the

◀ *Julian (L) and Lincoln (R) with the recovered bell in 2012. Reproduced with permission of Norfolk Historic Shipwrecks Ltd.*

Multiple Sclerosis Society. Our late mother Linda had been diagnosed with the condition in the late 1980s. We have had many more adventures together and separately, including circumnavigating mainland Britain by sea in six days with a group of good friends to support the same charitable cause. Julian also rowed across the Atlantic to Barbados with friends, and this turned out to be a record-breaking crossing completed in thirty-three days. Lincoln was unable to join this challenge because we were in the midst of relocating our printing business Barnwell Print Ltd.

When we found the *Gloucester* in 2007, our father was on board our survey boat with our great friend and diving partner Tiny. Although Dad never got the chance to dive the wreck site, it was special for him to be with us after so many years of searching. Tiny is still involved in the project and has been instrumental to getting it to its current stage. We always say that one of the best parts about this journey was meeting and working with Tiny.

Do you feel a particular connection to any of the objects you have found?
We both feel a real connection to the *Gloucester*'s bell. Not only is the bell the heart of the ship, but we also always imagine how it was ringing as the *Gloucester* sank. We were both diving together when Lincoln found it. When we make presentations about the *Gloucester*, we very much enjoy revealing the actual bell to people as their reactions are a joy to watch. To date all we have rescued are at-risk surface artefacts which on this dynamic site are exposed to environmental factors and the impact of fishing.

Meet 'Tiny': Interview with James Little

▲ *James 'Tiny' Little, October 2022.*

What is your role in the finding of the *Gloucester?* How did you become involved?

I met the Barnwell brothers in 2005, shortly after I returned from rowing solo across the Atlantic, having taken time off from running my Norwich pub and Lowestoft marine survey business. As I was carrying out maintenance work on my survey vessel the *Dornoch*, Julian and Lincoln walked across the gangway and asked if we could have a chat over a cup of tea. They told me the story of the *Gloucester*. I was immediately fascinated and joined the team, excited at the thought of another maritime adventure.

I began regularly meeting up with Julian and Lincoln in the middle of the night on their boat the *Penetrator* to catch the tide to the survey site and we would then return exhausted in the evening. We would take the *Dornoch* out between trips to dive possible target sites for the *Gloucester* which had been suggested by our survey work. It was on one of the final dives of the season in 2007 that we discovered the wreck site.

What did you feel like when the wreck site was located?

Relieved, elated, and with a strong feeling that the tough work was about to begin. The search that day had been laborious and tedious, and the foul weather meant we were in low spirits. Julian was out of action with an injury, and I drove the boat. Mike and I tended the divers Lincoln and Andy. When Lincoln surfaced with the news the mood switched to utter joy and we grinned the whole way back to Lowestoft.

Do you feel a connection with any particular object or objects from the wreck?

As a publican the wine bottles recovered from the site are of particular interest. I especially like the bottles with seals that have owner's initials or marks on them.

How has your work on the *Gloucester* changed your life?

My life changed from the moment the brothers crossed the gangway of my ship. It has been eighteen years of hard work, high and low spirits, great friendships, and meeting some truly amazing people. I have learned so much from the research and conservation experts we have worked with and I'm still learning.

What do you think should be done with the *Gloucester* wreck going forward?

I believe that we have the opportunity to bring the story of the *Gloucester* and the remains of the wreck to the world as an outstanding historical and heritage asset. The educational potential of the discovery is limitless. To date, we have only rescued artefacts which have been exposed by the tidal streams. There remains an enormous amount at the site still to be retrieved. In my heart, I would like to see a full excavation and lifting of the remains. I sat in a small boat in the Solent and watched the *Mary Rose* being lifted and that experience has stayed with me ever since. There is so much to be done with the *Gloucester*, this is just the beginning. ∎

Seventeenth-Century British Politics: Civil Wars, Commonwealth, and the Restoration of the Monarchy

The mid seventeenth century was a turbulent time in British history, with a long and bitter civil war fought between Parliament and the Stuart monarchy of King Charles I (1600-49) over political and religious control. In fact, the 'English Civil War' as it is known, was really three wars, the first two (1642-46 and 1648-49) fought between Parliamentarians, called 'Roundheads', against the 'Cavaliers' who supported Charles I and believed in rule by absolute monarchy and the principle of the divine right of kings. Roundheads wanted supreme control over the running of the country to rest with Parliament and freedom of worship for its people, rather than having to accept the authority of bishops and forms of worship insisted on by the Church of England. The Roundhead army won both of these wars, and after much debate between the army and Parliament over what to do with the king, Charles I was tried and executed on 30 January 1649 as a 'tyrant, traitor, murderer and public enemy'.

The monarchy was replaced with the Commonwealth of England. A third civil war (1649-51) was fought between Charles II (1630-85), the son of the executed king, and Parliament, but it too ended with victory for the Roundheads. Charles II was exiled, setting up a ramshackle court in mainland Europe: a king without a kingdom. The Church of England became Presbyterian.

From 1653, the British Isles was politically unified under the personal rule of Oliver Cromwell (1599-1658), a principal commander of the army and a Puritan, as the Commonwealth of England, Scotland, and Ireland. Cromwell was given the title of Lord Protector. Cromwell's use of the military to acquire political power and the brutality of the regime's campaign in Ireland mean he remains a controversial figure in British and Irish history. The *Gloucester* frigate, commissioned in 1652 as part of a shipbuilding programme to strengthen the navy, and launched in 1654, was originally a Commonwealth warship rather than a royal vessel. It was named after the Siege of Gloucester, which took place between 10 August and 5 September 1643 during the First Civil War when Charles I's forces failed to subdue the Parliamentarian stronghold.

◀ *Oliver Cromwell, Robert Walker, c.1649. This picture is over two metres tall, almost a life-sized portrait, and shows Cromwell dressed as a senior cavalry officer and carrying a general's baton of office. Courtesy of the Cromwell Museum, Huntingdon.*

When Cromwell died in 1658, his son Richard (1626-1712) briefly ruled the Commonwealth as Lord Protector (1658-59), but the resulting political crisis led to Parliament inviting Charles II to return from the continent to be restored as king. On Charles II's thirtieth birthday, on 29 May 1660, the king arrived back in London, promising leniency and tolerance under his rule, and to cooperate with Parliament. Together, the new king and Parliament reversed many of the Commonwealth's political, religious, and social policies. Not only was the monarchy restored but religious non-conformity was discouraged, and Anglicanism under the Church of England was re-established as part of the Clarendon Code, a series of legislative acts to ensure Anglican dominance in matters of church and state.

▲ *Charles II of England in Coronation Robes, John Michael Wright, c.1671-76. Charles II is dressed in Parliament robes over the Order of the Garter costume, wearing the Crown of State, the Sword of State, the Garter Collar with the Great George, and holding the new orb and sceptre made for his coronation. The king is shown seated under a canopy of state embroidered with the royal arms, in front of an armorial cloth of honour, with a tapestry depicting the Abduction of Romulus and Remus partially visible behind. Royal Collection Trust / © His Majesty King Charles III 2022.*

In fact, under Charles II, court life was flamboyant and known for its excess. Although Parliament voted the king an estimated annual income of £1,200,000, Charles was perpetually short of money since his revenues were paid in arrears. Expensive foreign wars and his hedonistic lifestyle and generosity to friends resulted in mounting debts. Theatres and music, fashion, and libertinism characterised the king's court. Charles II fathered many illegitimate children with his mistresses, including his oldest natural son James Crofts (1649-85), later Duke of Monmouth and Buccleuch, but none with his wife Catherine of Braganza (1638-1705), a Portuguese princess, who suffered a number of miscarriages. As a result, Charles' heir to the kingdom was his younger brother James, Duke of York and Albany (1633-1701).

▲ *King Charles II, reigned 1660-85, and King James II and VII, reigned 1685-88, unknown artist, c.1675, shown shaking hands, indicating their close relationship and shared interests in securing the Stuart succession. © Image; Crown Copyright: UK Government Art Collection.* ■

The *Gloucester* was built and launched during the First Anglo-Dutch War (1652-54), a conflict fought between the two countries over trade and overseas expansion. Since the war took place predominantly at sea, the Commonwealth Navy expanded at an unprecedented rate. Before Cromwell and the Parliamentary regime came to power, English monarchs rarely claimed ownership of more than fifty warships, yet in excess of two hundred vessels were added between 1649 and 1660.

◀ *Model of a warship; third rate; 58 guns, c.1650-55. © National Maritime Museum, Greenwich, London.*

To strengthen the navy, a major building programme of eleven warships was ordered in December 1652, contracted to both state-owned and private dockyards. The *Gloucester* was constructed at the private dockyard in Limehouse run by the Graves brothers, an established family of shipwrights. It was designed as a 'speaker-class' frigate, named after the *Speaker*, a fifty-gun warship constructed in 1650. Built by Matthew Graves (1608-81) the *Gloucester* was launched in the spring of 1654.

By March 1654, Benjamin Blake (1614-89) had been appointed as the *Gloucester*'s first captain. He was the younger brother of Robert Blake (1598-1657), the most famous and skilled British commander of the day. Since the war against the Dutch ended in April 1654, the *Gloucester*'s first active service was as part of the 'Western Design', an expedition against the Spanish Empire in the Caribbean. In December 1654, the ship sailed as part of a fleet from Portsmouth to Barbados. The expedition's assault on the island of Hispaniola (today the Dominican Republic and Haiti) was rebuffed by Spanish forces, although British forces seized the smaller island of Jamaica. The mission was viewed as a catastrophic failure

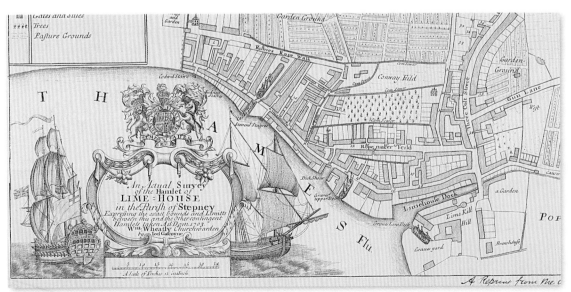

▲ *Map of Limehouse showing Graves' dockyard, 1703. Joel Gascoyne, image © London Metropolitan Archives (City of London).*

▲ *The three younger children of Charles I, James, aged fourteen; Elizabeth (1635-1650), aged twelve; and Henry, aged eight; Sir Peter Lely, 1647. © National Trust Images.*

for the Cromwellian regime, especially as many people died from yellow fever and other diseases. The *Gloucester* remained in the Caribbean until the autumn of 1656, when it returned home before participating in operations off Spain, Portugal, and the North Sea.

Cromwell's death in 1658 and a debt-ridden navy led to the *Gloucester*'s reduced operational use. It was laid up 'in ordinary', in other words the ship was secured with only a small skeleton crew rather than active at sea. After the Restoration, the Commonwealth Navy was renamed the Royal Navy. Charles II inherited a large debt from an almost bankrupt state and his naval arsenal remained securely anchored, with the *Gloucester* laid up at Portsmouth. Both Charles and his brother James, Duke of York, were naval enthusiasts. Before stepping foot on English soil at his restoration, Charles renamed many warships that held anti-monarchical titles. Vessels were renamed to reflect the royal succession, with the *Marston Moor* called the *York* for instance, though the *Gloucester* retained its name probably because the king's youngest brother, Henry, was the Duke of Gloucester (1639-60).

In 1664, the *Gloucester* was refitted for active service as political tensions with the Dutch Republic re-emerged. The *Gloucester* participated in several major battles of the Second Anglo-Dutch War (1665-67). Commanded by Captain Robert Clarke (died 1669), it took part in the Battle of Lowestoft in June 1665 and the Four Days Battle in June 1666, fought partially off the Suffolk coast. The latter was especially gruelling, with almost twenty per cent of the *Gloucester*'s crew injured or killed. Under Captain Richard May (dates unknown), it participated in the St. James' Day Fight a month later.

▲ *The Battle of Lowestoft, Adriaen van Diest, c.1690. With the burning hull of the Dutch ship Eendracht visible in the right foreground, the carved and gilded English flagship Royal Charles dominates the scene, cannon blasting and sails billowing. Gift of the Berger Collection Educational Trust, 2020.3. Photography courtesy Denver Art Museum.*

After the conclusion of the Second Anglo-Dutch War in 1667 and having experienced fifteen years at sea, in 1669-70 the *Gloucester* was extensively refitted at Portsmouth. Off the Isle of Wight in March 1672, the *Gloucester* was part of a squadron of ships that attacked a Dutch convoy returning from the Mediterranean. The incident led to Charles II officially declaring war on the Dutch Republic. The *Gloucester* was an active combatant in the Third Anglo-Dutch War (1672-74). Under the command of Captain William Coleman (died 1681), it was present at some of the largest and most deadly naval battles of the seventeenth century, including the Battles of Solebay in May 1672 and Texel in August 1673. During the Battle of Solebay off North Suffolk, James, Duke of York, led the English fleet as Lord High Admiral. He was forced to move flagships twice after his vessels the *Royal Prince* and *St. Michael* received damage, while the newly built *Royal James* of 102 guns was destroyed after being rammed by Dutch fireships.

The *Gloucester* was heavily damaged during the battle, requiring new fore and main masts and its hull was also leaking. The ship was patched up and returned to sea but when a peace treaty was signed in February 1674, it was clear that more significant repairs were needed.

Instead of immediately undergoing repairs, the crown resorted to decommissioning many of its warships to save money, including the *Gloucester*. This work was delayed until 1678 when the ship was brought into dock at Portsmouth and received a refit that took almost two years to complete. Its gundeck was almost entirely newly laid, with new wooden beams provided for the orlop, upper, and quarter decks. The ship's bulkheads, head, galleries, and stern were made almost entirely new. The ship was made watertight by caulkers, carvers added ornate wooden decorations, and glaziers fitted glassworks, while a new furnace was installed. In short, the *Gloucester* underwent a major refurbishment, and, in many ways, it was a new ship on the voyage to Scotland in May 1682.

'His Royal Highness the Duke of York is very zealous to engage the Dutch, God sending a good opportunity and water enough under our keels'.
Captain Richard Haddock on board the Royal James near Solebay, 21 May 1672.

▲ *The Burning of the Royal James at the Battle of Solebay, 7 June 1672, Willem van de Velde the Younger, 1675. Het Scheepvaartmuseum, Amsterdam.* ■

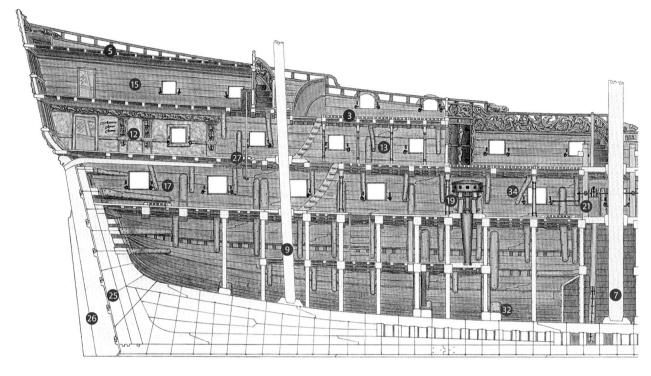

1 Gun deck	7 Main mast	13 Steerage
2 Upper deck	8 Fore mast	14 Forecastle
3 Quarterdeck	9 Mizzen mast	15 Roundhouse
4 Forecastle deck	10 Bowsprit	16 Cook room
5 Poop	11 Hold	17 Gunroom
6 Platforms	12 Great cabin	18 Belfry

▲ *Cutaway of the Gloucester as it looked in 1682, annotated with its main features, by Richard Endsor, 2022. Reproduced with permission of the University of East Anglia.*

In this section, in order to understand the structure and layout of the *Gloucester*, we introduce some of the principal design features of a seventeenth-century warship.

Captain's cabin or Great cabin ⑫

The largest and most extravagantly decorated room on the ship. It included a bed for the captain and a table for the officers to use to dine and meet. In May 1682, James, Duke of York would have occupied this space and the *Gloucester*'s captain, Sir John Berry (1636-90), would have been housed in a smaller cabin.

Officers' quarters ❸ ⑮

The quarterdeck was chiefly assigned as officers' cabins. The ship's lieutenants and master would have a room here, although because of the *Gloucester*'s elite passengers in May 1682, these cabins almost certainly would have been offered to the guests.

Capstan ⑲ ⑳

A rotating mechanism used when hauling ropes and cables and for lifting heavy items. The jeer capstan was located on the ship's waist on the main deck, but also extended down to the gun deck. A second capstan also worked the anchors and was located behind the mainmast on the gun deck.

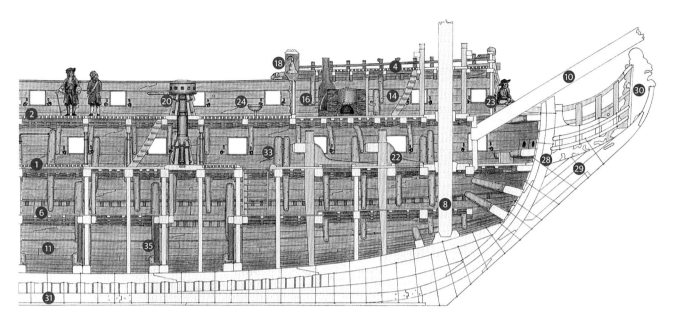

19 Main capstan	25 Stern post	31 Keel
20 Jeer capstan	26 Rudder	32 Riders
21 Chain pumps	27 Whipstaff	33 Standards
22 Riding bitts	28 Stem	34 Knees
23 Seat of ease	29 Head	35 Cross pillars
24 Pissdale	30 Figurehead	

Galley or Cook room 16

The ship's kitchen, which housed the furnace. Fire on a wooden structure was a major hazard and the galley was normally placed on the main or upper deck behind the foremast to help manage the risks from potential outbreaks. The galley included a double copper furnace placed on top of a hearth constructed out of bricks and tiles. A copper chimney positioned over the furnace released the heat and smoke the furnace produced.

Head and figurehead 29 30

The ship's head marked the front of the vessel and supported the figurehead. For Restoration warships, the figurehead was a carved lion.

Whipstaff 27

The whipstaff was a large vertical pole on the main deck used to move the rudder.

Pump 21

Two mechanical pumps rotated to remove any seawater found at the bottom of the ship. Using an iron chain, the mechanism would raise the water vertically and release it out of the ship.

Riders and standards 32 33

Structures used to reinforce and strengthen older ships. Riders were internal frames fitted to the widest part of ships to bind the two sides of the hull together. Standards were curved L-shaped wooden pieces known as 'knees' placed between deck beams and the ship's sides to alleviate strains from the ship's weight.

◀ *Ship's bell, inscribed with the maker's mark 'WW' and the date '1681'.*

Bell ⑱

The ship's bell was placed in a belfry at the waist of the ship and the bell played an instrumental role in the ship's daily running. It was central to the ship's operation because it was used to signal the watch: one stroke of the ship's bell indicated the first half-hour of the watch, then an additional bell was struck for each succeeding half hour. Eight bells indicated the end of a four-hour watch. The bell was also key to the *Gloucester*'s discovery. Its recovery in 2012 with its '1681' date mark decisively determined that the wreck found by the Barnwell brothers and their team was indeed the *Gloucester*.

Size and armament of the *Gloucester*

By the 1650s when the *Gloucester* was built, warships were divided into 'rates' according to tonnage, number of guns, and the size of the crew. First rates were the largest vessels. They carried around one hundred heavy guns, positioned across three decks. These ships served as the flagship of a fleet. As first rates were costly to equip and operate, they were few in number and almost never employed outside of war. In contrast, sixth rates were the smallest warships in the navy, with fewer than twenty guns and fifty crew members. Smaller ships were the most economical options and regularly commissioned by the navy in times of both peace and war.

The *Gloucester* was a third-rate warship, making it one of the larger vessels in Charles II's Royal Navy. Yet as it was smaller than the first and second rates, it was more likely to be commissioned outside of war, as occurred in May 1682 when the *Gloucester* was the largest vessel of the squadron transporting the Duke of York to Scotland. Though third rates were armed heavily, their size made them nimble and manoeuvrable when sailing. In 1673, there were nine first rates, nine second rates, twenty-three third rates, forty fourth rates, twelve fifth rates, and ten sixth rates in Charles II's navy. Whereas Henry VIII's flagship the *Mary Rose* had a keel that measured 105 feet, the *Gloucester*'s was 117 feet. Along with its hold, the Stuart warship featured orlop deck, gun deck, main deck, and quarterdeck. In 1682, it was recorded with a crew of 270 seamen.

◀ *Sketch probably of the Gloucester in c.1673, Willem van de Velde the Elder. Collection Museum Boijmans Van Beuningen, Rotterdam; Credit line photographer: Bob Goedewaagen.*

Although its armament fluctuated, the *Gloucester* carried between fifty and sixty guns. In 1677, the warship was assigned sixty guns in times of war and fifty-two when at peace. At war, its gun complement consisted of twenty-four cannon that fired twenty-four lbs shot, twenty-four demi culverins, ten light sakers, and two guns firing three lbs shot. The ship was a heavily armed floating fortress. In preparation for its final voyage, the *Gloucester*'s guns were heaved aboard the ship in late April 1682; it was standard practice to unload heavy weaponry from ships when they were not operational to preserve the structural integrity of the hull. When James, Duke of York boarded the *Gloucester* on 4 May 1682, Captain Berry was reported as having ordered the firing of a full broadside of twenty-seven guns to welcome him, suggesting the ship carried at least fifty-four pieces of heavy artillery when it was wrecked. Archaeological remains from the *Gloucester* shipwreck show that the ship was well armed when it sunk despite being extremely crowded with crew and passengers.

The Design of a Stuart Warship

▲ *Julian and Lincoln Barnwell measuring cannon. Reproduced with permission of Norfolk Historic Shipwrecks Ltd and the Maritime Archaeology Trust.*

At least twenty cannon have been visible on the shifting sandbanks since the discovery of the wreck site in 2007, and it is anticipated that more than thirty remain submerged under the sands. Most of the weapons are likely to be made of cast iron, although brass, a more expensive commodity, was also occasionally used.

A warship in active service was a lively and dynamic environment. The crew were continuously operating the rigging, cleaning, checking the ship's course and the depth of water, amongst other duties. Below deck, its crew experienced dark and smelly conditions while seeking spaces to rest, eat, and entertain themselves. Most of the crew slept on hammocks, with the gun deck serving as a communal area for relaxation when they were not on duty. Many of the ship's officers had their own cabins with the captain, lieutenants, and master all expecting to have an area to store their belongings and to sleep. These small rooms were found on the quarterdeck, but they also featured on other decks as well. The ship's surgeon, purser, carpenter, and their stores, were likely to have been located on the orlop deck.

Living conditions on board the *Gloucester* in May 1682 would have been uncomfortable for both passengers and crew, since it was overcrowded with people, cannon, and the extra baggage carried by its passengers. Accommodating the Duke of York, along with his large retinue of followers would require many of the officers to give up their cabins. ■

Maritime Art and Royal Patronage

When Charles II was restored to the throne in 1660, the influence of European style was evident in many aspects of Stuart court culture. This included an admiration for Dutch maritime art, widely acknowledged to be the most accomplished at the time, perhaps because of the importance of seafaring to the Dutch Republic. Dutch maritime art transformed the medieval Christian tradition of portraying the sea from a bird's eye view and as symmetrical, reflecting the organization of the heavenly cosmos. Instead, Dutch artists often painted using a horizontal point of view, with a lower horizon and a greater focus on realism than symmetry.

Both King Charles and James, Duke of York, were passionately interested in the sea and in expanding the English navy, seeing it as central to the nation's success at home and abroad. They commissioned paintings of seascapes to reflect the dignity and power of the monarchy. The brothers also loved sailing, building up a fleet of yachts, which they used as pleasure craft for racing, entertaining, and diplomatic voyages.

▲ *An English ship on the high seas caught by a squall, known as 'The Gust', Willem van de Velde the Younger, c.1680; this warship is in distress since a fierce gust of wind has broken one of its masts and a sail has come loose. Rijksmuseum, Amsterdam.*

The most notable of the Dutch artists were Willem van de Velde the Elder (1611-93) and his son Willem van de Velde the Younger (1633-1707). In 1673, at Charles' request, the father and son relocated to England. They were given a studio in the Queen's House in Greenwich Palace and a salary of £100 a year each. This was the start of a stable and lucrative association with the Stuart royal house which lasted thirty-five years. The pair often worked collaboratively, creating royal commissions, producing

▲ *English royal yachts at sea, in a strong wind in company with a ship flying the royal standard, Willem van de Velde the Younger, 1689. © National Maritime Museum, Greenwich, London.*

magnificent paintings, and designing tapestries of naval battles and seascapes; they produced thousands of detailed sketches, drawings, and designs of vessels.

Willem van de Velde the Elder was the son of a barge master and from an early age had accompanied his father at sea. He became a notable ship's 'draughtsman', often recording ships and battles first-hand in his sketches. These drawings could later be worked up into his trademark, highly accurate 'pen paintings', where he ground a canvas with white oil paint before drawing on it with blue India ink. Willem van de Velde the Younger followed in his father's footsteps, training as a painter to become the most celebrated maritime artist of his day. His seascapes captured some of the sea's more elusive features, such as light and shadow, or the reflection of the sky over the ocean's uneven surface.

Notable not only for depicting naval battles and documenting politically and diplomatically important seascapes, the Van de Veldes' work also captured the Stuart royal family's delight in yachts. The Van de Veldes' studio established maritime painting as an important strand of British art and cultural identity. Knowledge of Dutch methods of maritime painting was considered so fundamental that it was likened to 'grammar school' for later British maritime artists. ∎

Trade, Empire, and the Stuart Monarchy's Role in the Slave Trade

Between 1500-1800, European nations established colonial and imperial domination over many regions and peoples across the world. At the end of the sixteenth century, England began attempting to build an overseas empire to rival Spain in the west (in the Americas) and the Ottomans in the east. By the mid seventeenth century, the Dutch had established a powerful and lucrative maritime mercantile empire, through the activities of the Dutch East India Company, a chartered joint stock company established to trade in Asia. To increase England's presence within the global economy, extend state power overseas, and create revenue for the crown, in 1660 Charles II and City of London merchants set up a mercantile trading company, the Company of Royal Adventurers Trading to Africa. It was led by James, Duke of York as Governor, who was also its largest shareholder.

▲ *Coat of arms of the Royal African Company. © Museum of London.*

While the Company's original purpose was to exploit the gold fields up the Gambia River, supplying gold and ivory to England, it soon developed a brutal slave trade along the west coast of Africa, shipping Africans to the West Indies and the Americas. Before the Restoration, the Dutch had been the main suppliers of enslaved people to England's Caribbean plantations, but the Stuart monarchy aimed to oust them from this lucrative trade and establish England's monopoly over it. In 1664, Fort James (named after the Duke of York) was founded on an island up the Gambia River as a new centre for English trade and power. Over the next decade, the English and Dutch captured, lost, and recaptured the forts that served as their trading stations. This turbulence led to financial difficulties, and the English trading company was reconstituted as the Royal African Company, or RAC, in 1672, with new charters and fresh investment. As Dutch control of the region diminished, RAC trade generated significant profits for the crown and its investors. African gold, ivory, and money from slavery were used to finance the Stuart regime.

▲ *This 1687 Guinea coin dates from after the Duke of York had ascended the throne as James II. The inclusion of an elephant and castle motif on the bottom edge of the coin, taken from the RAC's coat of arms, indicates that the gold came from the Guinea region in Africa and was imported into England through the Company. Private Collection.*

By the 1680s the RAC was on average transporting about 5,000 enslaved people to markets primarily in the Caribbean each year. In 1682 alone, it transported over 13,000 people with 3,000 dying in transit. Many enslaved Africans were branded on their chests with the letters 'DoY', for the Duke of York, while others were branded with 'RAC'. Investors were fully aware of its activities and intended to profit from this exploitation. Edward Colston, whose statue was recently removed in Bristol, was a major investor and senior figure in the RAC from 1680. ■

The Exclusion Crisis and Catholicism: the Motives for the Duke of York's Voyage to Scotland on the *Gloucester*

Since Charles II fathered no legitimate heirs with Queen Catherine of Braganza, his brother James, Duke of York, was his heir presumptive. In the early years of his reign, Charles enjoyed a productive relationship with Parliament and wide public support. By the mid-1670s a series of problems and issues – the Great Plague of 1665, the Fire of London in 1666, expensive wars with the Dutch, and Charles' unpopular alliance with the Catholic King Louis XIV of France (1638-1715) – resulted in a more fractious relationship between the king and the commons. In particular, the disastrous and expensive Second Anglo-Dutch War (1665-67), instigated by the Duke of York, significantly decreased popular support for the king and his coterie. The war had been sparked by the duke's ambitious belief that England could defeat the Dutch in a naval war in the Channel and North Sea, even suggesting to his brother that it would be self-financing through the English navy's regular capture of Dutch East India ships laden with valuable goods. In fact, the king was forced to hastily conclude peace in July 1667 after the Dutch Medway Raid in June where, humiliatingly, the navy was unable to prevent two English warships being captured, towed, and sailed in triumph as prizes to the United Provinces.

Charles' toleration of Catholicism created tensions with Parliament. Queen Catherine was Catholic, his brother James and his first wife Anne Hyde (1637-71) secretly converted to Catholicism in 1668 or 1669, and Charles too was suspected of having agreed to convert to Catholicism to secure financial subsidies from Louis of France. Though Charles sought to suspend penal laws against Catholics and other religious dissenters, who did not want to worship according to the Anglican practices of the Church of England, Parliament opposed this and instead obliged Charles to agree to introduce the Test Act in February 1673. This legislation required those holding public office to receive the Christian sacrament under the forms set by the Church of England, and later forced them to denounce the Catholic belief of transubstantiation in the Eucharist.

◀ *James Stuart, Duke of York and Albany, in garter robes, school of Peter Lely, c.1650-75. Bolton Library & Museum Services, Bolton Council.*

The Exclusion Crisis and Catholicism: the Motives for the Duke of York's Voyage to Scotland on the *Gloucester*

▲ *Mary of Modena, studio of Peter Lely, undated; wife of James, Duke of York, later King James II and VII, she reigned as Queen of England and Scotland 1685-88. The Bodleian Libraries, University of Oxford, LP211.*

After the introduction of the Test Act, James' Catholicism became widely known when he refused to take the sacrament according to the Church of England. As a result, the duke was debarred from holding public office and, in June 1673, was forced to resign his position as Lord High Admiral of England. In addition, James' second marriage in September 1673 to the fifteen-year-old Italian Catholic Princess Mary of Modena (1658-1718), indicated to his Protestant countrymen his enduring commitment to the Roman faith. Protestants suspected that Mary was determined to bring about the conversion of England, making her and her husband unpopular. Whatever the nature of his private beliefs, Charles publicly opposed his brother's conversion, ordering that James' daughters, Mary (1662-94) and Anne (1665-1714) – both were to become Queens of England – be raised in the Church of England.

James' Catholicism provoked a major constitutional crisis between 1678-81 when a Protestant group called the Country Party, later termed the Whigs, attempted to exclude him from inheriting the throne.

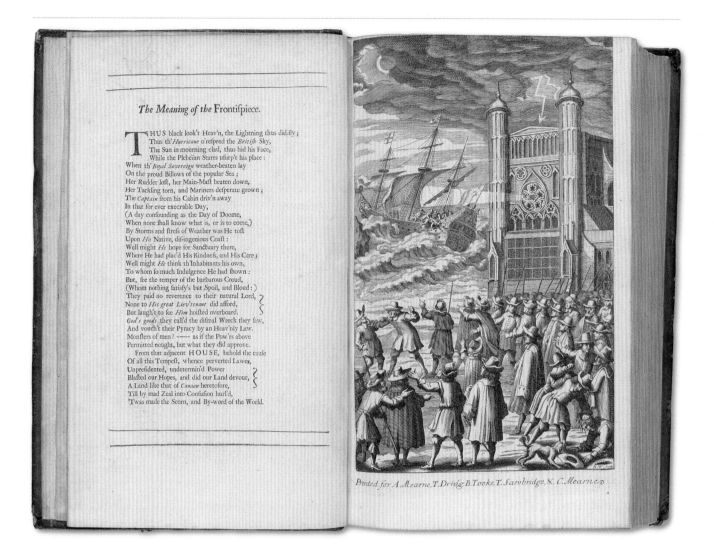

The Meaning of the Frontispiece.

THUS black look't Heav'n, the Lightning thus did fly;
Thus th'*Hurricane* o'refpred the *Britifh* Sky,
The Sun in mourning clad, thus hid his Face,
While the Plebeian Starrs ufurp't his place:
When th'*Royal Sovereign* weather-beaten lay
On the proud Billows of the popular Sea;
Her Rudder loft, her Main-Maft beaten down,
Her Tackling torn, and Mariners defperate grown;
The *Captain* from his Cabin driv'n away
In that for ever execrable Day,
(A day confounding as the Day of Doome,
When none fhall know what is, or is to come,)
By Storms and ftrefs of Weather was He toft
Upon *His* Native, dif-ingenious Coaft:
Well might *He* hope for Sanctuary there,
Where He had plac'd His Kindnefs, and His Care;
Well might *He* think th'Inhabitants his own,
To whom fo much Indulgence He had fhown:
But, fee the temper of the barbarous Croud,
(Whom nothing fatisfy's but Spoil, and Bloud:)
They paid no reverence to their natural Lord,
None to *His* great *Liev'tenant* did afford,
But laugh't to fee *Him* hoifted overboard.
God's goods they call'd the difmal Wreck they faw,
And vouch't their Pyracy by an Heav'nly Law.
Monfters of men! —— as if the Pow'rs above
Permitted nought, but what they did approve.
From that adjacent HOUSE, behold the caufe
Of all this Tempeft, whence perverted Lawes,
Unprefidented, undetermin'd Power
Blafted our Hopes, and did our Land devour,
A Land like that of *Canaan* heretofore,
Till by mad Zeal into Confufion hurl'd,
'Twas made the Scorn, and By-word of the World.

Printed for A. Mearne, T. Dring, B. Tooke, T. Sawbridge, & C. Mearne.

▲ *John Nalson (1638?-1686). An impartial*
◄ *collection of the great affairs of state, from the beginning of the Scotch rebellion in the year MDCXXXIX. to the murther of King Charles I (London, [printed for A. Mearne, T. Dring, B. Tooke, T. Sawbridge, and C. Mearne], 1683), leaf pi2 recto: engraved frontispiece. Call #: N106 Vol. 2. Used by permission of the Folger Shakespeare Library.*

The Exclusion Crisis and Catholicism: the Motives for the Duke of York's Voyage to Scotland on the *Gloucester*

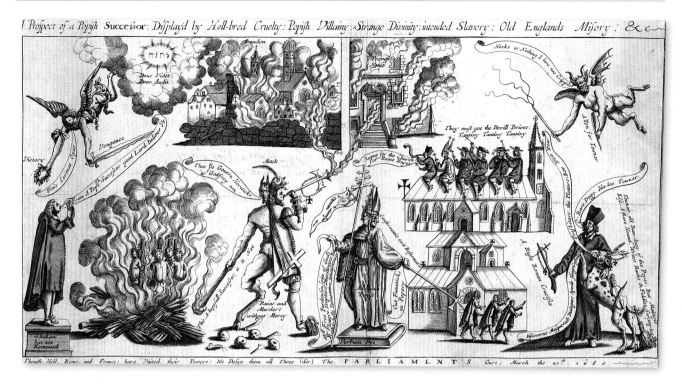

▲ *A Prospect of a Popish Successor by Mack-Ninny, 1681. This popular satirical print shows James, Duke of York as half-devil and half-papist, revealing the depths of his unpopularity.* ©The Trustees of the British Museum. All rights reserved.

Led by Anthony Ashley Cooper (1621-81), 1st Earl of Shaftesbury, they feared that a Catholic king would be the puppet of Louis XIV, making the nation subservient to France. In 1679, the House of Commons introduced the Exclusion Bill, which sought to debar the Duke of York from the line of succession. To prevent it becoming law, Charles was forced to dissolve Parliament. At the same time, there were a number of conspiracies, real and imagined, concerning plots to murder Charles and replace him with his brother. Most prominently the 'Popish Plot' (1678-81) to kill the king, provoked mass hysteria and led to a number of executions. Some even sought to confer the crown on the Protestant Duke of Monmouth, Charles' eldest illegitimate son. As a result, James was increasingly vilified and fearing the overthrow of his own rule, Charles ordered James and his family to leave the court, to reside first in the Hague and then in Scotland, where the duke mainly remained from 1679-82.

After the threat of the Exclusion Crisis to the Stuart succession began to subside and the royalist party, the Tories, were ascendent in Parliament, Charles invited his younger brother to return to England. Initially, in March 1682, James had returned alone, via East Anglia and Norwich, and following a warm welcome from the court and subsequently the City of London, he was invited to return to court permanently. On 4 May 1682 he departed by sea to Scotland in the *Gloucester*, accompanied by a small fleet, to collect his family and settle royal affairs in Edinburgh. His wife Mary was pregnant at the time, and it was hoped that the new baby would be a boy to secure the Stuart succession and be born in England. ∎

Navigation and the North Norfolk Sandbanks

Naval ships like the *Gloucester* carried many instruments to help officers and crew to navigate, such as compasses, backstaffs, hour glasses, sounding leads, and dividers. The Board of Admiralty Commissioners received a request in September 1673 to supply the *Gloucester* with 'meridian compasses', for instance, and records also survive from 2 May 1682 of John Hull, the ship's boatswain, confirming delivery of a consignment of 'half hour glasses'. Both were essential instruments for navigation, with the compass enabling mariners to know their direction of sailing and sandglasses used to measure the time spent on a course.

▲ *A seventeenth-century thirty-minute glass filled with speckled ochre sand and a mariner's compass, mounted in a turned wooden box. © National Maritime Museum, Greenwich, London.*

Officers were expected to provide their own portable professional equipment, including navigational tools such as dividers, often personalised with initials or other identifying marks. Used by mariners to measure distances on charts, mark a ship's position, or plot a course, several pairs of dividers have been rescued from the *Gloucester* wreck site.

Ships also employed a pilot to manoeuvre through dangerous waters, who knew the depth, currents, and hazards of waterways. The *Gloucester*'s pilot was Captain James Ayres (dates unknown), a mariner experienced in navigating the waters around Norfolk and personally known to the Duke of York, having served with him with distinction in 1672 at the Battle of Solebay.

Determining location at sea with precision remained a challenge for mariners. There was no accurate way of measuring longitude until John Harrison (1693-1776) invented the marine chronometer in the eighteenth century. Until then, though sailors used charts and navigational tools to determine location, they preferred navigating within sight of land where landmarks were used as points of reference.

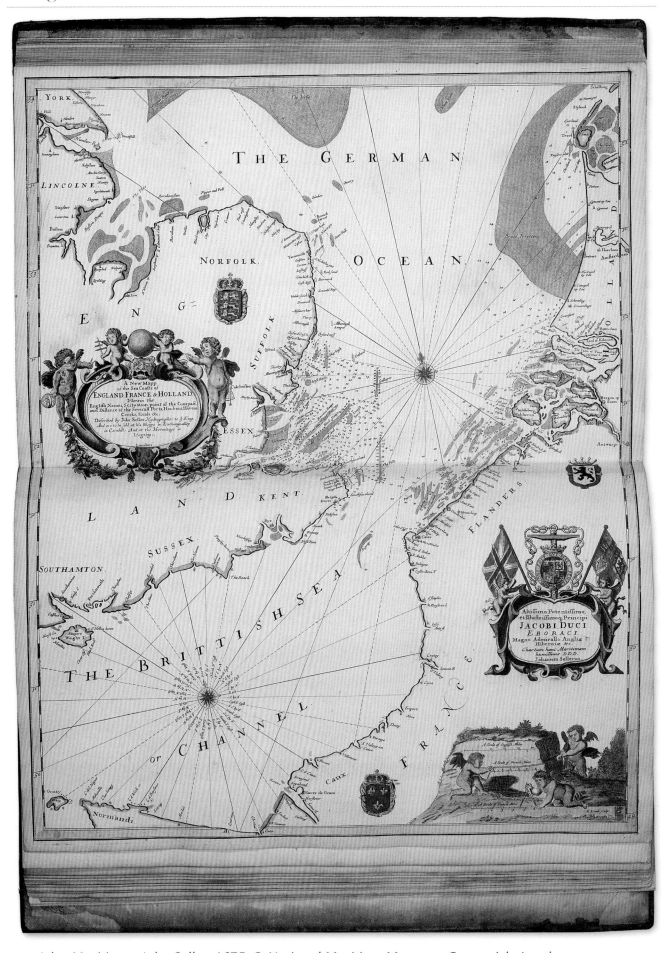

▲ *Atlas Maritimus, John Seller, 1675. © National Maritime Museum, Greenwich, London.*

One of the main difficulties the *Gloucester* faced on the night of 5 May 1682 was navigation. As officers plotted a course along the Norfolk coast, the ship needed to pass a number of treacherous sandbanks. The North Norfolk Sandbanks extend from about forty kilometres (twenty-two nautical miles) off the coast to 110 kilometres (sixty nautical miles) and comprise the Leman, Ower, Inner, Well, Broken, Swarte, and four banks called, collectively, the Indefatigables. Out of sight of land, the officers and the Duke of York disagreed over the best course to take to avoid them. Should they carefully pick their way through them using charts, hug the coast in order to navigate by landmarks, or sail far out to sea to avoid them altogether? Hidden by the water, could they even tell where they were? These sandbanks were notoriously difficult to navigate because the channels between them were dynamic, as claimed by Ayres after the *Gloucester* struck a sandbank.

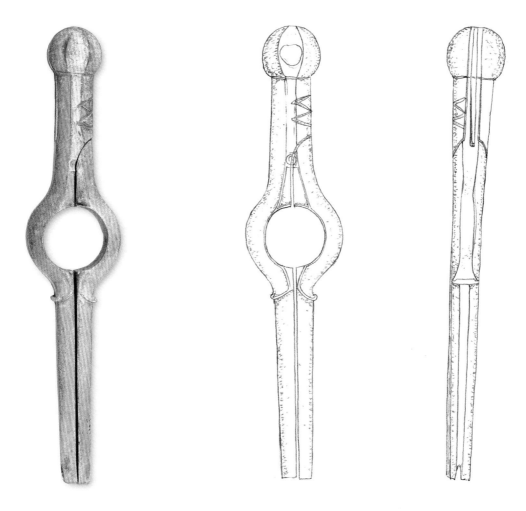

▲ *Personalised navigational dividers, rescued in 2008 from the Gloucester wreck site. Reproduced with permission of Norfolk Historic Shipwrecks Ltd.*

Another problem the *Gloucester* faced was the lack of accurate maritime charts of British coastal waters. The map on the previous page, *A new mappe of the sea coast of England France and Holland* was published in 1675 in *'Atlas Maritimus', or the Sea Atlas* by the royal hydrographer John Seller (1632-97). It includes a dedication to the Duke of York, and Seller hoped to produce a maritime map that would rival those of the great Dutch cartographers. But the map showed the sandbanks on which the *Gloucester* foundered in the wrong place, only about fifteen miles from land. ∎

What Happened on 6 May 1682?

On the evening of 5 May an argument took place concerning the best route to enable the fleet to clear the North Norfolk sandbanks on its journey north. It involved the *Gloucester*'s pilot James Ayres, senior officers including Captain Sir John Berry and Master Benjamin Holmes, Captain Christopher Gunman and Captain Ralph Sanderson, respectively of the *Mary* and *Charlotte* yachts, and James, Duke of York. Ayres, experienced in sailing the coastal route, advocated sailing between the coast and sandbanks, the so-called 'Colliers Road'. Holmes, without local knowledge, supported a deep-sea route beyond the sandbanks, the standard course taken by big ships heading north. James, a former Lord High Admiral of England, and an experienced naval commander in these waters, argued for a middle path between the two routes. The duke's route was eventually agreed upon, and the pilot was instructed to follow it. According to Berry, at 4am Ayres 'presuming and confident, affirmed that this course would carry the ship out of all danger, and that we were past the Lemon and Oare'. Ayres then went to bed. The *Gloucester* hit sandbanks at approximately 5.30am on 6 May.

◄ *Captain Sir John Berry, Michael Dahl, c.1689. Berry wrote a narrative of what happened on the Gloucester immediately after the wreck. Philip Mould & Company © Philip Mould Ltd, London/Bridgeman Images.*

As the ship sank within an hour, and because most people were in bed at the time, there was no time to organise an evacuation. James delayed leaving, hoping that the *Gloucester* could be saved. Under pressure from his advisors Captain John Churchill (1650-1722) and Colonel George Legge (1647-91), James was forced to abandon ship shortly before it sank via the window of the stern cabin. His rescue boat was deliberately underfilled. Since protocol dictated that others on board could not abandon before royalty, only two further ship's boats had time to launch. One swiftly overturned in the rough sea and the other, overcrowded, narrowly avoided sinking. The scene was chaotic: 'all the seamen and passengers were not at command, every man studying his own safety' reported Sir James Dick (1644-1728), Lord Provost of Edinburgh, in a letter written on 9 May 1682. It is estimated that between 130 and 250 people drowned.

'I stood in upon the sand, and went close to them, when the ship drove off from the sands into fifteen fathoms of water, where she went to the bottom, some part of her topmast being above water'.
Christopher Gunman, Letter written to his wife Joy from Leith Road, 9 May 1682.

▲ *Sketch in 'Captain Gunman's Cause', annotated 'The postures wee were in stering NNW the wind at E: Runing after the Rate of 9: leagues a watch The sand Trenching NW: & SE: the Glocester E by S of me when I came on the Deck: about ½: a mile distance', Dartmouth Papers, Staffordshire Record Office. Reproduced courtesy of Staffordshire Record Office and the Dartmouth Heirloom Trust.*

This previously overlooked sketch drawn by Captain Gunman shows what happened. It plots the courses that the *Gloucester* and the *Mary* and *Charlotte* yachts followed and shows their positions relative to the sandbank. It also records the depth of water measured in fathoms (one fathom = 1.8 metres). To get into deeper water after finding his ship in nine fathoms, Gunman shows the *Mary* changing direction to sail west as well as the course it took after the *Gloucester* struck the sandbank, when it mounted a rescue effort. ∎

Who was to Blame? Courts Martial

Even though James, Duke of York survived the wreck and completed his journey to Scotland on the *Mary* yacht, identifying who was to blame for such a major tragedy was a significant political and naval question. As a result, two courts martial were held in June 1682 to determine responsibility. The first, held on 6 June 1682 on the *Charlotte* yacht, was brought against the *Gloucester*'s pilot, Ayres, presided over by Sir Richard Haddock (1629-1715), the newly appointed Comptroller of the Navy and Commander in Chief of all His Majesty's Ships and Vessels in the River Thames and Narrow Seas. Though Ayres was condemned to life imprisonment, he did not serve the full sentence since a year later, on 5 June 1683, Charles II ordered his release. This sentence of imprisonment was handed down despite James' expectation, as revealed in a letter to William of Orange, that Ayres would receive his 'doom' through execution.

The evidence presented by Gunman at the case against Ayres led to accusations of misconduct being made about him. A week later, on 13 June, a second court martial was held against Gunman and his first mate, William Sturgeon (dates unknown), for failing to follow admiralty orders requiring a ship to warn adequately accompanying vessels of impending danger. Since the *Mary* was sailing ahead, strictly speaking it was required to alert the *Gloucester* of shallow water by firing a gun. Gunman admitted that he had ordered flags to be waved instead, as he claimed was normal. He was found guilty of misconduct though Sturgeon was acquitted. Gunman was imprisoned, fined, and dismissed from his post. Haddock presided at this trial as well.

▲ *Admiral Sir Richard Haddock, John Closterman, c.1700. Courtesy of the National Museum of the Royal Navy.*

Gunman was furious. He claimed that witnesses who gave evidence against him had also attempted to intimidate others into giving false testimony about his neglect of duty. Gunman suggested that there was a conspiracy against him, alleging that Haddock was prejudiced. No direct evidence survives to support these claims about Haddock, though he spoke favourably of Ayres' skills as a pilot whilst identifying Gunman as culpable for the wreck. Recent research has uncovered evidence of attempted witness tampering against Gunman, but who arranged it remains a mystery.

One reason Gunman might have been scapegoated was his close relationship with the Duke of York, who was known to be reliant on him. It is possible that by convicting Gunman a message was being communicated to James concerning royal interference in the navy. The return of James to political

◄ Captain Christopher Gunman, unknown artist, c.1675. Doddington Hall & Gardens, Lincolnshire.

▼ Court Martial of Captain Christopher Gunman, Richard Endsor, 2022. This painting by Richard Endsor imagines how the court martial of Christopher Gunman (seated, right foreground), captain of the Mary yacht, might have looked. Held on 13 June 1682 on board the Charlotte yacht at Greenwich, Gunman is shown being questioned by Sir Richard Haddock (standing, centre) as President of the board, which also included Captain Henry Williams, Captain George Churchill, Captain Thomas Allin, Captain William Botham, Captain Matthew Tennant, Captain Ralph Wrenn, Captain George St Loe, with Henry Croom as Judge Advocate. Reproduced with permission of the University of East Anglia.

power in the London court was likely to shake-up naval policy and senior admiralty officers feared that he was likely to attempt to influence future strategy. Gunman did not languish in prison for long, however. James intervened on his behalf and Charles II reinstated him to his role as captain of the *Mary* yacht within ten days. ■

Given James, Duke of York's position as heir presumptive, newspapers swiftly published accounts of the *Gloucester* shipwreck. With a number of notable individuals on board, reports of who died and who survived were national talking points, with palpable relief amongst pro-Stuart Tories that James had survived. Countrywide celebrations were encouraged including the ringing of church bells, firing of cannon, and bonfires.

Details of what happened were sketchy initially, with the first brief published account appearing in *The London Gazette* on 8 May, followed by a more detailed summary on 11 May by Captain Berry. His account suggests that even as the crew were themselves drowning, they patriotically celebrated James' rescue: 'the great Duty and Concern which the poor seamen had for his Royal Highness's preservation, was most remarkable'.

The Tories made political capital about James' survival. The composer Henry Purcell wrote an Ode, 'What Shall be Done in Behalf of the Man', celebrating the duke's personal qualities and the playwright John Dryden composed 'Prologue to the Dutchess, on Her Return from Scotland' to honour Mary of Modena's presence at the theatre and her husband's survival. A commemorative medal was issued aiming to capitalise on the relief amongst Tories that James had survived. The reverse shows a ship in distress off a rocky lee shore, towards which a boat approaches, and is inscribed 'IMPAVIDUM. FERIUNT.' meaning 'They strike him undismayed'.

◀ *Commemorative medal including image of the*
▼ *Gloucester shipwreck and bust of James, Duke of York, George Bowers, 1682.© National Maritime Museum, Greenwich, London.*

John Churchill was one of the officers defending James' rowboat from desperate wreck victims. Churchill served as the duke's Gentleman of the Bedchamber, giving him intimacy with the heir to the throne. James rewarded him for his service later in 1682 by making him Lord Churchill of Eyemouth. Churchill's outfit displays his royal connections since a redcoat was the uniform of the Stuart household, with identical uniforms worn by the duke's servants in Johan Danckerts' (1616-86) picture (see overleaf). The crowdedness of the rescue boat contradicts contemporary accounts that often focus on it being empty.

▲ *John Churchill, later 1st Duke of Marlborough, John Riley, c.1685-90.*
  Reproduced with permission of Blenheim Palace.

▲ *The Wreck of the Gloucester off Yarmouth 6 May 1682, Johan Danckerts, c.1682.*
© *National Maritime Museum, Greenwich, London.*

Not all commemorations were wholly celebratory. This painting by Danckerts shows an apparently romanticised version of what happened, capturing some of the key ambiguities about the tragedy. It shows the *Gloucester* beached, though survivors' accounts say the sandbank was covered with three fathoms (5.4 metres) of water. Three sailors are praying on the sandbank, whether for deliverance or in thanks for their salvation is unclear. One figure is scrambling ashore, while other crew and passengers

abandon ship. The proximity of an extensive sandy beach suggests all may still be saved. In the left foreground, a densely packed ship's boat, containing the duke, fishes further survivors from the water on its port side. Simultaneously, to starboard officers draw their sword and axe to attack those trying to clamber aboard, as the boat rows towards the waiting fleet in a calm sea. James sits apparently impassively in the stern. ■

Early Salvage Attempts

As the *Gloucester* sank so quickly, passengers and crew abandoned ship without their personal possessions. Sir James Dick wrote a few days later on 9 May that he 'was in my gown and slippers lying in bed when she first struck and escaped [...] in that condition'. Most people ended up in the sea where they either drowned or were fished out by the rescue boats which were despatched by the royal yachts accompanying the *Gloucester*. The passengers' and the crew's belongings – ranging from clothes and personal care items, through cutlery and wine for personal consumption, to professional and business items – were all lost with the vessel. Some accounts suggest James' 'extremely weighty' strong box was loaded into his rescue boat, but little else was saved.

Over the summer of 1682, Charles II ordered his royal yachts to search for the castaway *Gloucester* hoping to salvage items including 'some of the Dukes Plate'. Captain Gunman's account corroborates the loss of James' dinner set, as the duke was forced to eat off Gunman's own two silver plates on the *Mary* yacht for the remainder of the journey to Scotland.

◄ *Samuel Pepys, the 'Harwich' Portrait, attributed to Marcellus Laroon the Elder, c.1685. The famous diarist was also Secretary of the Admiralty from 1673 to 1679, and 1684 to 1689. He witnessed the sinking of the Gloucester in May 1682 from the accompanying royal yacht Katherine. By permission of the Master and Fellows of Magdalene College, Cambridge.*

This silver plate belonged to Samuel Pepys and is marked with the date 1671 © Museum of London. ▶

'the Duke came on board just with a coat and breeches on, which was all he saved, – plate, linen, clothes, money, etc., all gone to the value of above £5,000'.
Christopher Gunman, Letter written to his wife Joy from Leith Road, 9 May 1682.

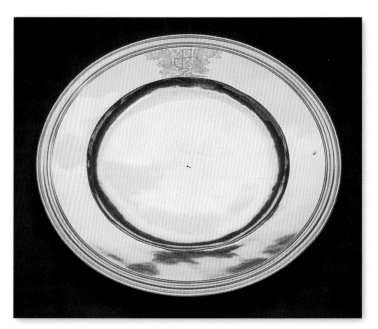

It was not just lost possessions that those on board or their relatives wanted to recover. Lady Margaret Ker (c.1657-1753), the widow of Robert Ker, 3rd Earl of Roxburghe, on hearing the news of her husband's death organized a search party to recover his body. Roxburghe (c.1658-82) was one of the most notable casualties and was just twenty-three or twenty-four at the time. He was still undressed in his cabin at the time of the ship's sinking. James had called for Roxburghe to come on board his rescue boat, but he could not be found. Instead, the earl, offering without success 20,000 guineas for a boat, was forced to jump into the sea. Since he could not swim, his servant James Littledale (died 1682), who was a more competent swimmer, took him on his back and swam towards one of the yacht's rowboats. Both however perished due to a struggle with another desperate wreck victim, who pulled them under water.

▲ *Lady Margaret Hay, Countess of Roxburghe, about 1657–1753, Gerard Soest, c.1675. National Galleries of Scotland. Accepted by HM Government in lieu of inheritance tax and allocated to the Scottish National Portrait Gallery 2005.*

▲ *Robert Ker, 3rd Earl of Roxburghe, Peter Lely, c.1675. Reproduced with permission from Roxburghe Estates.*

Lady Margaret ordered her servant, Alexander Ramsay (dates unknown), to travel down to Great Yarmouth to attempt the task of recovering her husband's body. He arrived on 14 May and worked with Sir Thomas Meadow (1624-88), bailiff of the town, to commission a local fisherman and navigation instrument maker, John Grice (died c.1703), to travel with Ramsay to the wreck site where the ship's mast was still visible above the waterline. They sailed to the site and for two or three days searched for the body, but with no success. Undeterred however, Ramsay proceeded to travel to all the seaports in and around Great Yarmouth, hoping to find news of the body being washed up on the shoreline, but Roxburghe's body was not found. Lady Margaret never remarried despite surviving her husband by seventy years. Later that summer Grice was successful in recovering some of the *Gloucester*'s rigging for the navy. ■

The *Gloucester* Wreck Site: Interview with Garry Momber, Director, Maritime Archaeology Trust

▲ *Garry Momber, Director of the Maritime Archaeology Trust. Garry has been awarded fellowships by the Society of Antiquaries and the Society of Underwater Archaeology, and obtained accreditation within the UNESCO Convention on the Protection of Underwater Heritage.*

Maritime archaeology is a specialised branch of the discipline of archaeology that studies human interaction with the sea, lakes, and rivers through the study of associated physical remains, be they vessels, shore-side facilities, port-related structures, cargoes, human remains, and submerged landscapes. When the Barnwell brothers and James Little first discovered the wreck of the *Gloucester*, the Barnwells took a course on maritime archaeology, but the team also sought expert advice at an early stage. They consulted Garry Momber, Director of the Maritime Archaeology Trust (MAT). During his thirty years in this field, working across academic, consultancy, and charitable sectors, Garry has led pioneering projects that have helped steer a course for the discipline, nationally and internationally, and has published extensively in academic journals. With his ambition to share the hidden secrets of the deep to make it more accessible, he has focused on research and interpretation. Making extensive use of evolving technologies, such as the technique of photogrammetry to survey the seabed and create 3D digital models, he actively promotes the relevance of the underwater cultural heritage within contemporary society. Here he discusses his involvement with the project and explains more about the nature, and complexities, of this unique site.

What is your role in the finding of the *Gloucester*? How did you become involved?

MAT became involved with the *Gloucester* wreck over five years ago when we were invited by Norfolk Historic Shipwrecks to advance the longstanding site investigations with a photogrammetric survey of the entire wreck site. We have visited the wreck many times to record the exposed ship structure and assess threats to the ongoing survival of the site. The results of the investigations over the last fifteen years will now be incorporated into a management plan that will chart a future course of action for the wreck.

Describe the wreck site. How large is it? What can you see, and how much is yet to be found? Has it changed much since you first saw it in 2018?

The wreck of the *Gloucester* is relatively compact as it sank quickly, landing upright on the seabed before steadily collapsing in on itself. The exposed elements of the shipwreck site and artefact scatter are now in the order of fifty metres long by twenty metres wide. Initial assessment of the site indicates that the wreck listed to starboard as it settled into the sandy seabed. In time, the decks collapsed and the cannon worked downwards, ending up scattered across the contents of the hold below. A large section of the port side of the hull now lies partly visible within the seabed, while the upper starboard side appears to have been lost. However, a drop in sand levels around the bow of around a metre in 2020 revealed planking that indicated a sizeable section of the starboard hull remains beneath the wreck mound. It is estimated that the deposit of artefacts along the centre of the wreck are in the order of two to three metres deep. Where they remain undisturbed they will be well protected, but dives on the site over the last five years have recorded the movement of sand across the site that both covers and uncovers material, putting all newly exposed artefacts at risk.

When diving the site, visibility is generally restricted to three to five metres, but the dominant features are the twenty guns lying on and within the sand. Most lie on top of an elevated linear mound that runs from the bricks of the galley fire hearth near the bow, back along the length of the ship towards the stern. This tracks above and adjacent to the line of the keel. In amongst these large features, the seabed is scattered with rope, ship's fittings, and the remnants of onboard activity. The items represent the surface expression of a seventeenth-century palimpsest of archaeological artefacts that have yet to be uncovered.

Who do wrecks belong to and what are you legally allowed to remove from the seabed?

In principle, shipwrecks belong to the person that owned them at the time of loss. In the UK, onboard items can be recovered as long as they are declared to the Receiver of Wreck in an attempt to find the owner where one still exists or the succession of ownership can be demonstrated. Historical wrecks, or those where there has been loss of life are often protected, thereby restricting access. However, this will depend on the jurisdiction within which they are found and the legislation of the nation state.

What is the difference between underwater archaeology and rescue or salvage archaeology?

Underwater archaeology is the study of underwater cultural heritage for the purpose of recording the evidence and saving the results for the benefit of humanity. Rescue for salvage is not archaeology but the recovery of the material for personal financial gain or repatriation with the owner.

What is photogrammetry and how is it used to enhance the interpretation of wreck sites? How much has technology changed a maritime archaeologist's role?

Photogrammetry is the process of taking and linking multiple photographs to create a scaled, digitised, three-dimensional model of the site. The results can be used to create a baseline survey of the site that can be studied to aid interpretation and inform management strategies. It can also be used for display and dissemination. Photogrammetry has enabled maritime archaeologists to create detailed surveys of sites in a matter of hours. See pages 50-51 for photogrammetry of the *Gloucester* wreck site.

As a maritime archaeologist, how significant is the *Gloucester* discovery and how should the site be managed? What are the key risks?

The *Gloucester* is an internationally important site that contains a rich resource of ship structure and personal items, that can tell us a great deal about an important period in British political and naval history. This makes it one of the most significant wrecks found around British shores to date. The remaining artefacts are incredibly rare, even potentially unique. Those that have survived due to being in an anaerobic (oxygen-free) environment will be very well preserved. Site management is a challenge. The continual exposure of artefacts on the seabed demonstrates that objects are being uncovered and then transported by the tide along the seafloor. These objects will invariably be lost. The loss of each item slowly diminishes the value and significance of the site. Threats also exist from fishing, as evidenced by the nets that have already been caught on the site, and by treasure hunters who could destroy the historical evidence while looking for high value objects. An assessment is underway to quantify the risks, along with methods that could stabilise and protect the site from these risks. If this is not possible, archaeological excavation would be the next best way of maximising the heritage value and saving the site and the history it contains for the future.

◀ *Divers regularly monitor and record changes to the Gloucester wreck site. Reproduced with permission of Norfolk Historic Shipwrecks Ltd and the Maritime Archaeology Trust.*

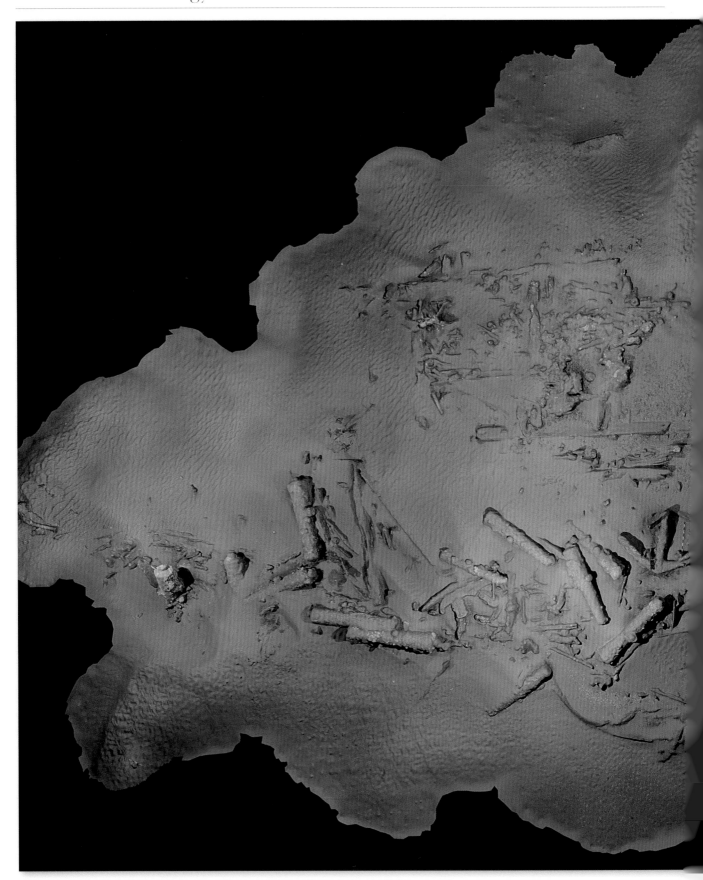

▲ *Photogrammetry carried out by Maritime Archaeological Trust, summer 2022, showing bow (R) and stern (L).* ■

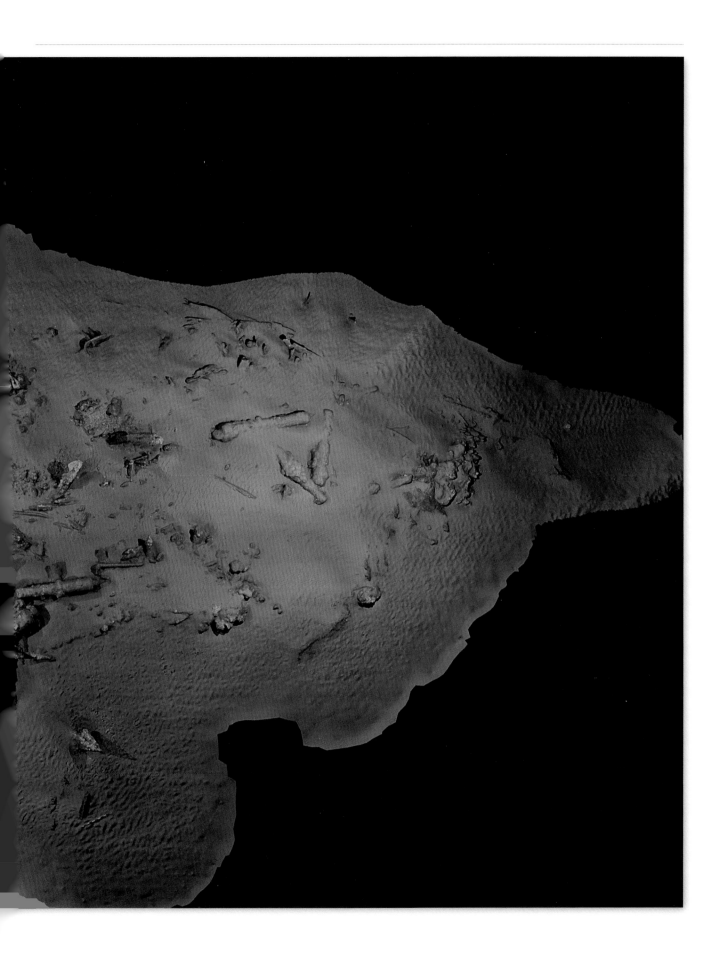

Conserving Artefacts Recovered from the *Gloucester* Wreck Site: Interview with Ian Panter, Head of Conservation, York Archaeology

▲ *Ian Panter examining an artefact rescued from the Gloucester wreck site. Reproduced with permission of the University of East Anglia.*

As soon as artefacts began to be recovered from the *Gloucester* wreck site, the most urgent priority was to ensure their stability. Even if objects were well-preserved while under the sea, once they are brought up into the air their condition deteriorates, often irreversibly, if appropriate steps are not taken. Julian and Lincoln Barnwell consulted conservators on preservation techniques. Later, the objects went for full conservation to York Archaeology. Here we speak to Ian Panter about the processes of conservation.

How did you first get involved with the *Gloucester* shipwreck? How does it compare with other maritime conservation projects you've worked on?

The Barnwell brothers first approached me in 2017 about conserving a wooden barrel stave and everything developed from there. York Archaeology have worked on several maritime projects, but the *Gloucester* assemblage includes materials we don't often get to work on. Usually we're dealing with wood, leather, and metals but finds from the *Gloucester* also include glass bottles, ceramics, and clay pipes.

What are the challenges of conserving artefacts that have been submerged in the sea over three hundred years?

Over the centuries, artefacts will have become waterlogged and saturated with harmful salts. Decay can make artefacts fragile, so they need careful handling and to be kept wet at all times until they reach the conservation laboratory. The challenge is to remove as much salt as possible before drying them. Composite artefacts (made from two or more materials) can be particularly challenging because treatment appropriate for one material may be harmful to another and compromises have to be considered.

What processes do you use? What is 'desalination' and why do you do it?

Desalination is the process whereby we remove as much of the harmful salts as possible. The most aggressive salt is chloride which if left *in situ* will promote corrosion and deterioration. Flushing out using copious amounts of water is the most basic technique, although for iron we may need to use an electrical current and a sodium hydroxide electrolyte to assist in the process. We can never really remove all the chloride from metals, but we try to reduce the concentration to safe levels (usually less than fifty parts per million).

Once desalinated, artefacts are dried. For metals and glass, we use solvents such as acetone. For organics like wood and leather, we use freeze-drying. This involves impregnating the artefact with a consolidant, which is a chemical that acts as a support for the decayed areas and prevents collapse of the artefact during drying. Artefacts are then frozen to around minus twenty degrees Celsius before a vacuum is applied. Under these conditions of reduced temperature and pressure, the water is first converted to a solid (ice) and then to vapour which then migrates from the artefact to a 'cold trap' which is typically held at minus fifty degrees Celsius. This process, known as sublimation, is a very gentle way of drying organic materials.

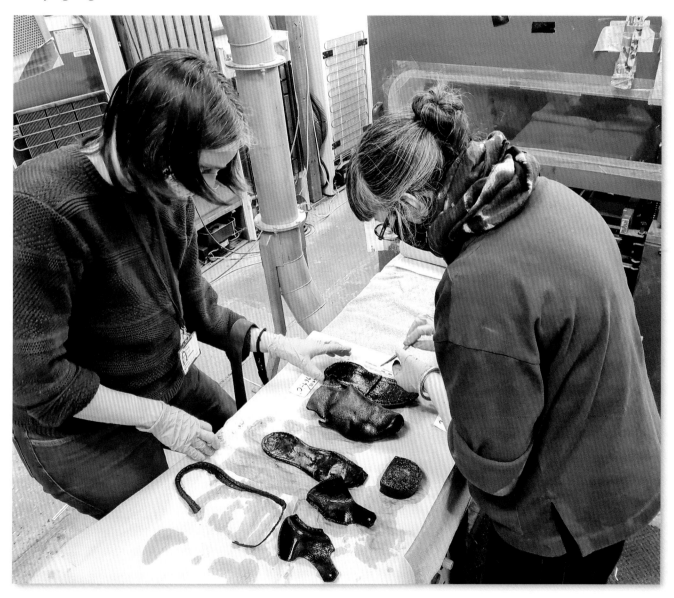

▲ *Norfolk Museums Service staff undertaking documentation on the leather shoes prior to conservation, May 2021.*

Conserving Artefacts Recovered from the *Gloucester* Wreck Site: Interview with Ian Panter, Head of Conservation, York Archaeology

▲ *Conservation in progress at York Archaeology.*

How long does it take to conserve artefacts rescued from the *Gloucester*? Can you save all the objects?

Conservation of artefacts from the seabed is a time-consuming process. Desalination cannot be speeded up without potentially causing damage. Leather and wood tend to take a matter of months to desalinate, whereas iron objects such as cannon balls can take a year or more depending on their state of preservation. Larger iron items such as cannon can take around three years to conserve. The next stages, consolidation and drying, can vary from a few weeks to several months, sometimes as much as a year for the larger wooden artefacts, whilst structural ship's timbers can take over two years to treat. We aim to conserve every artefact. There is nothing we cannot preserve, although we may need to specify the creation of tightly controlled storage or display environments.

Which items from the *Gloucester* have been the most difficult to conserve? Have you been surprised by the nature or condition of any of the finds?

Nothing so far has proved too difficult to conserve although some items are more of a challenge. For example, the horn combs are quite rare since horn doesn't usually survive well from shipwrecks. We research appropriate processes as well as carrying out small-scale experiments before we begin artefacts' conservation.

I am not surprised by the overall state of preservation of the finds from the *Gloucester*. We often see excellent states of preservation from waterlogged and saturated environments. It has been interesting to work on items that could be considered 'high-status' because of the passengers on board at the time of the wreck. We often work on 'everyday' or discarded objects, so the *Gloucester* artefacts are particularly interesting because of their context. ◼

▲ *A selection of the bottles rescued from the Gloucester wreck, including the bottle with the 'sun in splendour' glass seal.*

One of the most significant recoveries from the wreck site has been 149 rare seventeenth-century glass bottles. This is almost certainly the greatest number of wine vessels from the period ever discovered. The bottles' conditions vary from incomplete bottle necks to whole items. Many of the bottles remain sealed: forty-nine have internal contents and of these, twenty-nine have their airlocks (ullage) and liquids intact. Glasses rescued from the site show the type of receptacle passengers on board the *Gloucester* used for drinking wine. The finds are important for wine studies but also for historians as they raise a question – did drinking alcohol play a role in the tragedy? The number of wine bottles recovered suggests that the officers and passengers were drinking, perhaps excessively, to celebrate James, Duke of York's return to political prominence by being allowed by his brother Charles II to reside at court, but future archaeological, historic, and scientific research hopes to answer this question more decisively.

◀ *Close up of 'sun in splendour' glass seal. A number of taverns included the 'sun' in their names in the seventeenth century. Research is ongoing to establish the provenance of this bottle.*

◀ *Drinking glass recovered from the Gloucester wreck.*

English glass bottle making was a relatively new technological invention, having been patented by Sir Kenelm Digby (1603-55) during the 1640s. Wine was typically stored in casks, yet the production of glass bottles facilitated the transportation and distribution of wine, as shown by the bottles recovered from the *Gloucester*. Glass bottles were expensive, costing roughly four shillings a dozen, and were often reused.

Seven of the bottles recovered from the wreck have glass globular seals attached to their shoulder and are impressed with a seal matrix that served as owners' marks. Sealed bottles cost five shillings per dozen, a shilling more than plain bottles. Four of the *Gloucester*'s bottle seals use initials as an identifying trait such as 'WW' (see adjacent image) and 'ES', while others feature crests. The bottles with globular seals were expensive items that not only marked ownership but also often reflected high status. Sealed bottles were mainly owned by wealthy gentlemen and taverns. A sealed bottle could serve as a symbol of elite status, prosperity, or as branding. Tests to measure the capacity of seventeenth-century bottles have shown that on average gentlemen's bottles held approximately 950 millilitres, tavern bottles contained over one hundred millilitres less.

◀ *Bottle with 'WW' seal and its cork intact.*

The shape and style of the bottles, which are predominantly onion shaped – commonly referred to as shaft and globe in design – suggests that that they were older bottles and were probably being reused. The original shaft and globe shape produced since the 1640s evolved as the century progressed. The majority of bottles rescued from the *Gloucester* wreck have dark green complexions, and the wine they contained would have been young, since at this time wine had a shelf-life of about twelve months due to low alcohol content.

Glass Seals: The 'Coventry' Bottle

An outstanding example of a glass seal from the *Gloucester* wreck is the bottle rescued by the Barnwell brothers in July 2019 which bears a seal with three crescents, a fess ermine, and a coronet. In heraldry, a fess is a band running horizontally, an ermine is a symbol representing the winter coat of the stoat, and a coronet and crescent indicate rank within the nobility and a connection with monarchy respectively. The crest on this bottle suggests it is connected to the Barons of Coventry, a prominent Warwickshire family of the time, who were granted a coronet in heraldry by Charles II in 1661. Intriguingly, the coronet, which appears slightly worn on this bottle, does not clearly correspond to a baron's coronet, which is a circlet with four balls.

◄ *Wine bottle recovered in 2019 with detail of*
▼ *the glass seal, note the worn glass on the coronet.*

▲ *Memorial to John Coventry, 4th Baron Coventry, St Mary Magdalene, Croome, Worcestershire. PicturePrince, CC BY-SA4.0<https://creativecommons.org/licenses/by-sa/4.0>,via Wikimedia Commons.*

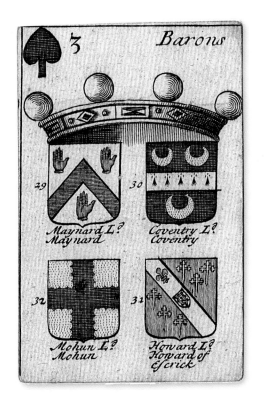

◄ *Arms of the Coventry family from 'Arms of English Peers' set of playing cards showing the coronet with four balls (1688).*

To whom might this bottle have belonged? In 1682 John Coventry (1654-85) was 4th Baron Coventry of Aylesborough. He had recently inherited the title from his father George Coventry (1628-80), the 3rd Baron, who had died in December 1680. Therefore, the bottle on the *Gloucester* in 1682 might conceivably have been originally owned by either George or John Coventry. The family were resident in Croome, Worcestershire.

Bottles with similar glass seals have been discovered before – one found in Worcester, and another is now in the collection of the Museum of London – and have been linked to the Coventry family. Neither of the glass seals on these bottles included a coronet. Recently, however, a cache of 'Coventry' bottles has been discovered by workmen a very short distance away from Coombe at Kinnersley, Worcestershire, and this group, like the *Gloucester* bottle, include a coronet on the glass seal. The coronets on the glass seals of the Kinnersley bottles

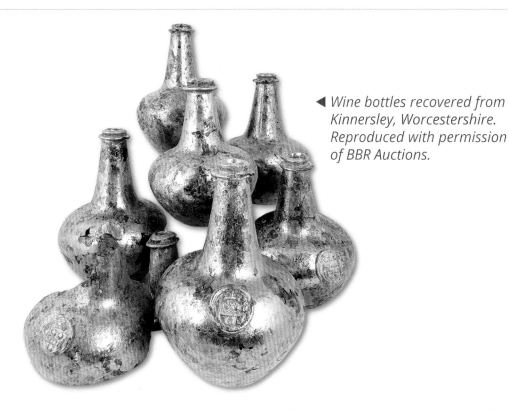

◀ *Wine bottles recovered from Kinnersley, Worcestershire. Reproduced with permission of BBR Auctions.*

appear very similar but not identical to the one on the *Gloucester* bottle: neither coronet is especially like a baron's coronet, but instead resemble a crest-coronet, the metal circlet without the heraldic chapeau or cap beneath. However, the use of differentiated coronets for the ranks in the peerage (in heraldry an earl's coronet is different to a duke's or to a baron's, for instance) was not fully established as a practice in the seventeenth century. As a result of this lack of differentiation in coronets at the time, it is likely that the coronets on the seals of both the *Gloucester* and the Kinnersley bottles do connect them to a member of the Coventry family, perhaps George or John, 3rd and 4th Baron respectively, or even to one of the extended family, such as William Coventry (c.1628-86), who had been closely associated with the Duke of York in the 1660s and 1670s.

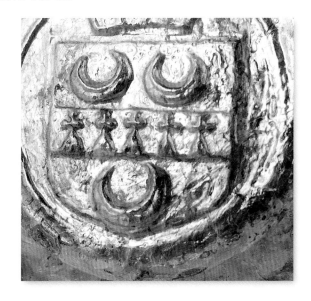

◀ *Close up of the distinctive 'Coventry' wine seal. Reproduced with permission of BBR Auctions.*

Further research is required to identify the owner of this bottle with certainty. Yet, given there were no known members of the Coventry family on board the *Gloucester* in May 1682, the recovery of this bottle from the wreck site raises intriguing questions about how wine bottles circulated at this time. ■

Seventeenth-Century Wine: Interview with Biochemist and Wine Scientist, Geoff Taylor, CChem CSci MRSC

How did you first become involved with the *Gloucester* shipwreck? Why was it important for a biochemist to be part of the research team?

My wine industry role has been a very specialized one for over forty years. During this time, I have analysed many tens of thousands of wines from across the globe including some from archaeological excavations and old cellars. Some of the wines tested were over two hundred years old. My work is well known throughout the wine industry and when the Barnwell brothers contacted a trade body, it was suggested they contact me. Biochemistry is the study of chemical processes relating to living organisms and my specialisation is microbial biochemistry. Wine is produced by the microbial transformation (fermentation) of grape juice. Detailed knowledge of this process and how the various compounds are formed and can change over time are essential prerequisites in assessing wines' provenance and quality.

What can biochemistry tell us about historic wine?

Wine is a complex product that can have over a thousand naturally occurring compounds. There are also well over a thousand different grape varieties and distinct styles of wines from the same variety. Each will have an individual chemical structure and will age differently. Wine chemistry is not static; as wine ages, new compounds are formed while others are broken down. How wine is stored can affect the chemistry. Once wine is bottled and oxygen is precluded, wine ageing and the chemical process of ageing slow down. Detailed knowledge of these variables, the chemicals involved in ageing, and which ones are markers for certain wine styles can only be gained from years of specialising in this area.

Given the amount of wine bottles rescued, some still sealed and with liquid contents apparently intact, is this a unique find?

This find is extremely rare. The large number of samples with an intact ullage (the air space between the base of the cork and the liquid) indicating the liquid has not been contaminated with sea water, is exceptional. We should not assume that every intact bottle contains wine: there was an occasion when an intact wine bottle from an archaeological dig contained urine which was hundreds of years old!

How do you analyse the properties of seventeenth-century wine?

The oldest wine I have previously analysed dates from the 1780s. That work was challenging. The bottles from the *Gloucester* are about a hundred years older but appear to be in better condition. There are a number of difficulties when analysing a wine of this age. The greatest is preclusion of oxygen since once oxygen has contact with the ullage air and/or liquid, then further chemical changes are likely to be rapid potentially destroying some compounds. Both the closure (cork) and glass are extremely fragile. Any air or liquid removed must be extracted into sealed, evacuated airtight containers. In view of the potentially small volumes available, it may not be possible to perform repeat analyses as is the norm in science. In short, you have to get it right first time. In order to maximise the data, some of the most sophisticated equipment will be used with the ability to detect compounds as low as the parts per billion level.

From your work to-date on bottles rescued from the *Gloucester*, how important might this discovery be to wine studies?

This research could provide a new insight into wine production and trade in the late seventeenth century. To date, I have analysed two bottles. Dissimilar bottle styles were selected in anticipation of finding different wine styles. The differences in data were significant. This could be a result of the wines ageing differently in the unusual and extended storage conditions. However, the divergences are so significant, I cannot envisage chemical pathways where this could have occurred unless the wines were of different origins.

What do initial tests tell us about the type of wine on board the *Gloucester?*

Analysis is at an early stage, but of the two bottles tested, we have two different wine styles. One sample has a high level of tartaric acid (the naturally occurring major grape acid), some glucose and fructose (the naturally occurring grape sugars), and a low alcohol content. The other has a much lower level of tartaric acid, more sugar, and more alcohol. Some gas chromatography-mass spectrometry work has also been performed which indicates different profiles. In view of the significant number of distinct bottle shapes and sizes, there might have been many styles of wine of different origin on the ship.

▲ *Geoff Taylor working with historic wine bottles.*

What else can the contents of these bottles tell us?

In addition to the liquid (wine) there is the air in the ullage. There will be wine derived compounds, but this 'air' is a sample of the atmosphere from the seventeenth century. It would be invaluable to have a comprehensive analysis of this air, in particular some isotopic analysis. ◼

Rescued Baggage from the *Gloucester:* Chests A and B

Many centuries-old artefacts survive because they are in the collections of museums or stately homes. They have been preserved because of their high monetary or cultural value. These items are often made of precious materials or are rare examples of an artist's work or an artisan's skill. This creates a vision of the past seen through items that were not in everyday use. The functional, well-worn possessions of everyday life can provide a fuller understanding of early modern lives.

Two wooden chests known as Chests A and B were discovered at the wreck site in August 2015. They were located close to a cannon and the bricks and tiles of the galley on the main deck's forecastle. Future excavation could determine whether the chest was originally located close to the galley and forecastle or may have been dislodged from another deck during the 341 years underwater. Both trunks are approximately ninety centimetres in length, forty-five centimetres wide, and sixty centimetres deep.

Since each chest had no lid, a programme of rescue archaeology was set in motion to save their contents from being lost to the shifting sand waves of the seabed. Just under one hundred artefacts were recovered over one summer dive season from Chest A or in close proximity. This chest was partitioned into a small and large compartment which contained diverse items, some high status, such as an expensive decorative glass-handled knife (see page 82), alongside a simple wooden spoon marked only with notches, probably to identify its owner. The transfer of baggage to the *Gloucester* off Margate is recorded to have taken several hours and this may have affected the packing of the chest. For instance, different individuals' luggage might have been packed together, or perhaps a servant's possessions may have been added to their master's (or less likely, their mistress') luggage. Viewed together, they offer a tantalising glimpse into the lives of some of the individuals on board.

▲ *Objects recovered from Chest A, including a pottery jug, leather pouch, spectacles in a wooden case, leather book covers, broken wine bottle.*

The layer of objects closest to the top of Chest A included a dark wooden jar and contents with a close-fitting lid. The wood is probably *lignum vitae*, a hardwood indigenous to South America and the Caribbean, known for its medicinal properties. The black substance inside the jar has been analysed and contains mustard grains, alum, and an aromatic compound probably derived from an essential oil extracted from thyme and known for its antimicrobial properties. Mustard was often applied as a hot poultice to treat joint pain and alum was widely used for medicinal purposes, including the treatment of skin ailments (see page 80).

◄ *Ceramic pot containing wax and shaft of a seal stamp, recovered from Chest A.*

Utensils for eating, drinking, and smoking comprise a quarter of the total number of objects found in or around Chest A. This group included three wine bottles, one with its cork and contents in place, a tankard made of wooden staves with a pewter lid, two pewter spoons, a stoneware jug, and sixteen clay pipes. Two small ceramic pots with pinched rims for pouring were packed in the topmost layer. One of these pots contains red wax, probably used to seal letters. An ornate brass shaft that held a seal stamp was in the chest, though the stamp itself has not survived. The presence of two pairs of spectacles, one complete and one just a pair of lenses, in a beautifully carved wooden box and three leather book covers suggests that the owner was literate and quite wealthy. Another leather artefact, a pouch with three crown stamps, indicates that its owner was likely a member of a royal household (see page 73).

A layer down in Chest A, a group of wooden items were packed together, which included a square frame used for winding yarn, two bobbins with multiple collars for storing thread, and several tool handles. The metal parts of the tools appear to have corroded away, but the shapes and sizes of the handles resemble those seen on awls and punches used to make holes, such as lace holes in leather shoes. A wooden shoe-last, shaped like a human foot and used by shoemakers, was also in this group of objects which suggests that the owner was engaged in making and maintaining clothing and footwear. A small disc from a lead cloth seal was in this chest (see page 67). These seals were attached to bales of cloth to identify the manufacturer or merchant, provide quality control, and a regulation system for taxation purposes.

Several double-sided combs were found, constructed with one wider set of teeth to detangle hair and a finer set to remove lice. There are four single combs, perhaps indicating that more than one person's belongings had been packed together, and a packet of six new combs. These were found still tied together with a length of braid and protective layers packed between each comb. This packet represents a rare find showing how new goods were wrapped, and hints that they were not required for the journey but had been picked up whilst away from home and transported with other luggage.

The Textile 'Bundle'

A tightly rolled bundle of textiles was rescued from the bottom of Chest A. The bundle revealed an assemblage of female apparel, with a pair of delicate leather shoes in the middle. Most of the items are made of fine silk, and although very fragile and in some cases fragmentary, the level of preservation is remarkable. This find offers a valuable opportunity to examine surviving clothing from the Stuart period. The contents include two silk skirts, which would have been called petticoats in this period. These garments were worn either with a matching bodice or under a long open gown with the outer skirt draped and pulled back to reveal the petticoat beneath.

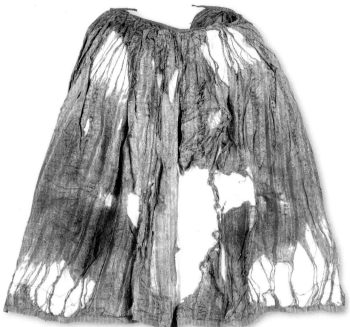

▲ *Silk petticoat with damask pattern of flowers and foliage.*

◀ *Illustration showing the vertical stripes of the design of the weave which is composed of symmetrical bands of plain, floral, and geometric pattern. Gwyneth Fitzmaurice.*

They are still intact, including their waistbands and the binding around the hem. The silk is damaged, but the quality and complexity of the figured floral and geometric patterns are still visible. Both petticoats have a vertical striped design in silk damask, which was fashionable from the 1670s to the end of the century. They are the same size, 56 centimetres (22 inches) around the waist and 82 centimetres from top to bottom, so they are almost certain to have been made for one person.

The other two complete garments are accessories, a soft, gathered silk hood and a cape collar with three sets of braids used as ties to close at the front. They are now a golden colour but were probably white or cream originally.

Hood, recovered from the textile bundle at the bottom of Chest A. ▶

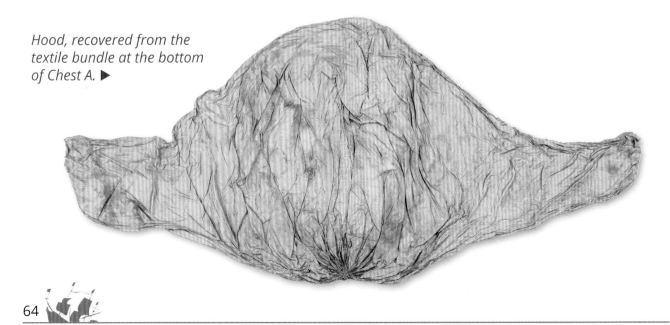

This style of hood was widespread during the second half of the seventeenth century. They are depicted in illustrations of fashionable attire, in portraits, and in interior scenes. The front edge of the hood would have been folded back several times when worn to ensure that the fine silk held a curved shape around the face. The silk has been finely pleated and precisely gathered into a tight circle to create the bag-like shape at the neck. The hood was fastened by tying together the two long edges at the front.

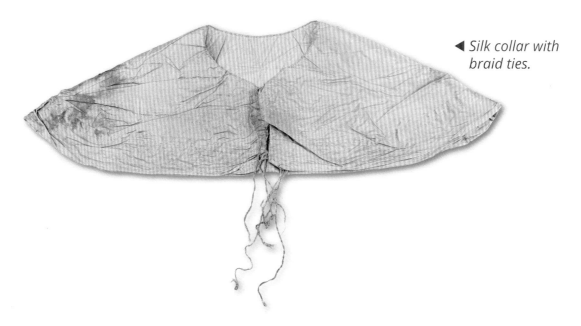

◀ *Silk collar with braid ties.*

The collar is plain, without any embroidery or evidence of stitch holes, showing that no trimmings or decoration had ever been attached. The collar is cut on the bias of the grain of fabric so that it hugs the curve of the shoulders with two small darts just behind the shoulder points to give a neat fit. Of the six lengths of braid that tied the collar closed, two – the top and bottom on the right-hand side – are a different type of braid, indicating replacement due to breakage or loss. From the evidence of wear and use on these garments, it is reasonable to assume they are from a person's wardrobe rather than gifts or newly acquired items. A group of thirty-seven copper alloy pins was found in the centre of the bundle. They would have been necessary to hold garments in place as part of an ensemble.

◀ *Order of procession for the coronation of James II (1685). This engraving shows the King's Herbs-woman and her maids and shows examples of the dress recovered as they would have been worn. © Historic Royal Palaces/ Robin Forster/ Bridgeman Images.*

Rescued Baggage from the Gloucester: Chests A and B

There were other textile fragments rolled up along with the more complete garments, adding to the picture of a set of clothing. Some of the smaller pieces are knitted and could have been parts of either stockings or a jacket.

▲ *Knitted fragment photographed and illustrated showing the stitches of a cuff, either the top of a*
▼ *stocking or the hem of a sleeve. Illustration Gwyneth Fitzmaurice.*

The pair of shoes at the centre of the bundle is in pieces but complete, with outer and inner soles, uppers, low wooden heels, and even leather heel covers. They are fashionable and well-made shoes with a high squared-off tongue, the two punched holes lining up with the latchet straps underneath for laces to be threaded through. Although narrow and small to the modern eye, they are the same size as other surviving examples of adult female shoes of the period.

The presence of this bundle is exciting. There is no confirmed presence of a female passenger on board the *Gloucester*. One account mentions an unidentified 'English Lady' who was reported as having drowned in the tragedy, but no other documents corroborate this. Perhaps the owner or owners of Chest A were transporting these garments for someone else? There are several pairs of male shoes in the chest but no other complete male garments. It is important to be cautious about drawing firm conclusions based on the objects recovered so far. Further research on this sensational discovery is required.

▲ *Parts of a woman's shoe recovered from Chest A with the upper parts on the top row and the wooden heel, leather heel cover, and sole parts underneath.*

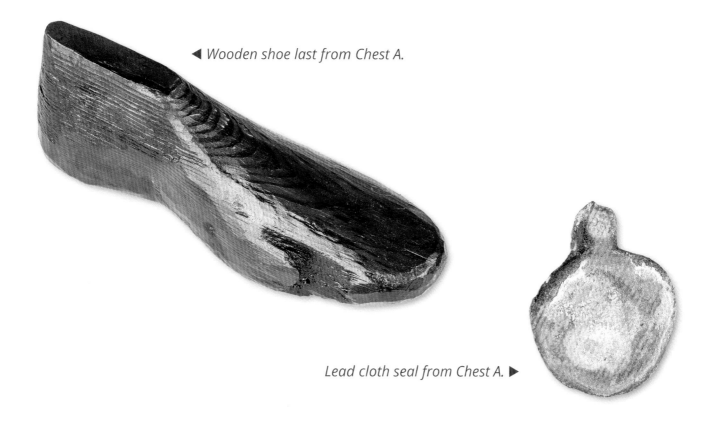

◄ *Wooden shoe last from Chest A.*

Lead cloth seal from Chest A. ▶

Chest B

Chest B was found located on the seabed between Chest A and a cannon, and it features a small corner compartment. Two wooden pins found in Chest B may have originally served as locking mechanisms for the chest's lost lid.

Forty-four artefacts were rescued from this chest, while four pipes and a wooden spoon were found in close proximity. It is possible that these items were originally contents of the chest. The artefacts recovered from Chest B suggest an owner or owners of wealthy and naval backgrounds. They include three wine bottles, two with liquid contents and airlock (ullage) intact, as well as three combs, an intact pair of well-made shoes with fashionable high heels, at least two leather book bindings, a number of other leather fragments, and four oyster shells.

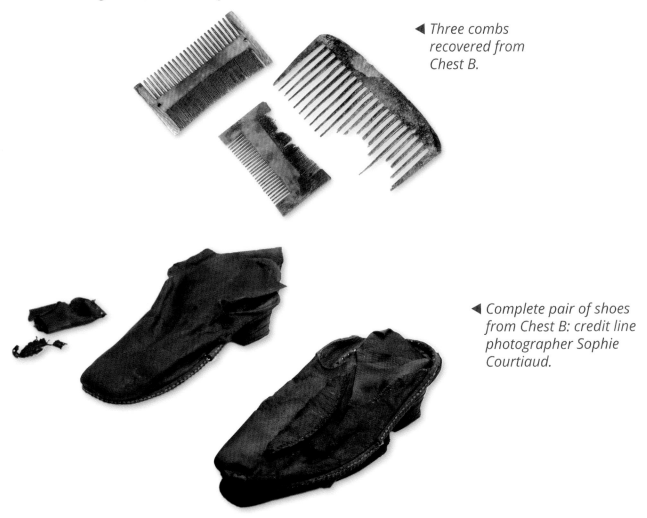

◀ *Three combs recovered from Chest B.*

◀ *Complete pair of shoes from Chest B: credit line photographer Sophie Courtiaud.*

Two pairs of brass navigational dividers were inside the trunk, but their steel pointers are missing. The maritime instruments suggest that the chest might have been owned by an officer with experience at sea or a gentleman with an interest in navigation. The leather book covers indicate that its owner was literate.

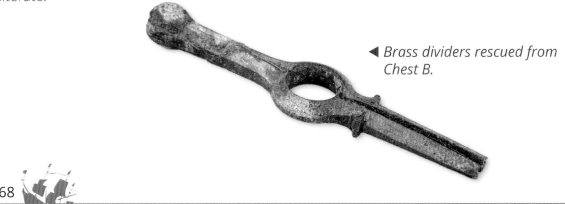

◀ *Brass dividers rescued from Chest B.*

Most significantly, a pace stick or dressing cane was recovered, resting diagonally in the chest from corner to corner. The wooden stick is approximately one metre in length with a copper alloy ferrule or cap at its base to protect the wood from wearing. Its knob was found detached in the chest and is silver and possibly gilded with gold. The stick connects Chest B to an individual of high status such as a gentleman passenger or a senior naval officer. In the seventeenth century, canes were designed to reflect social status rather than serving as mobility aids. Having a wooden cane with a silver knob reflected the wealth and importance of its owner.

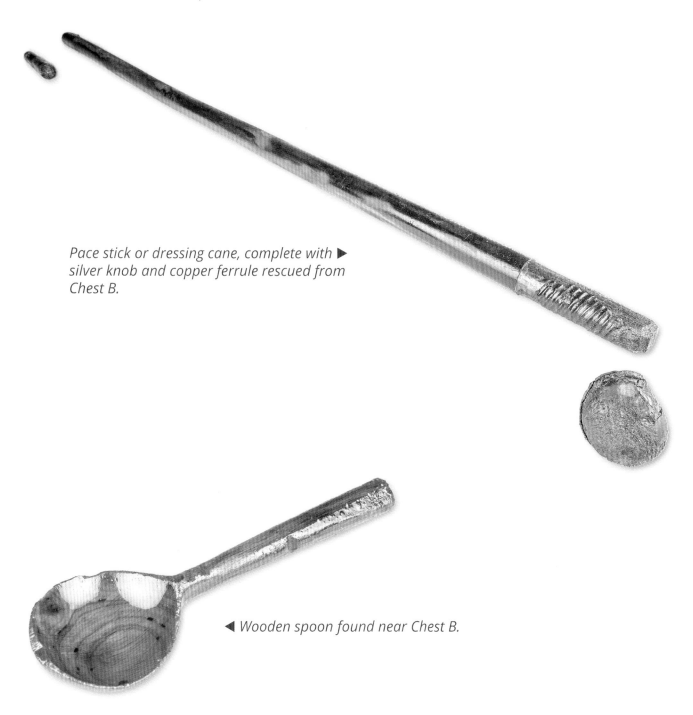

Pace stick or dressing cane, complete with ▶ silver knob and copper ferrule rescued from Chest B.

◀ Wooden spoon found near Chest B.

Taken together, the artefacts from Chest B indicate a gentleman owner or owners. It is possible that they belonged to one of the *Gloucester*'s officers, but it is also equally conceivable that they are the possessions of one of the elite or noble passengers interested in naval affairs. ■

How do we Interpret the Artefacts Rescued from the *Gloucester*? What can they tell us?

How do we go about understanding the significance of this group of artefacts rescued to date from the *Gloucester*? What evidence do these objects provide about the lives of the people on board or about what happened on the morning of the wreck?

Only rarely can we establish definitive links between an object and its owner, but many types of evidence suggest vital clues about social class or occupation. These allow us to interpret particular items and make intelligent connections. Some finds rescued to date can be convincingly associated with an individual or with a profession, such as medicine, but links between other objects are harder to establish. Processes of association are not straightforward. Survival of artefacts is unavoidably random, depending on the durability of materials and other circumstantial factors. In this case, recovery is also dictated by objects' locations, specifically whether artefacts were on the surface of the seabed. Rescue work of surface items about to be lost forever is the only archaeology that has taken place to date at the site. This is one reason why some items have been found in quantity and others not at all. For instance, nearly 150 wine bottles have survived, but only two fragmentary wine glasses. Likewise, spoons made of wood, pewter, and another metal alloy have been found, but none of silver.

▲ *Three pewter spoons found at the Gloucester wreck site.*

This sample cannot represent a balanced picture of the cutlery on the *Gloucester*. There must have been silver spoons, alongside less valuable utensils, because these are what the elite passengers would have used. Such a large quantity of wine bottles pre-supposes many more wine glasses. Nonetheless, these apparent anomalies can be explained: small items of silver could have been taken off the ship along with other portable valuables by their owners. Certainly, Sir James Dick, Lord Provost of Edinburgh, wrote in a letter written on 9 May 1682, just a few days after his own narrow escape from the ship in just his nightgown and slippers of 'having nothing saved but the twenty guineas which were in my little pocket with my watch, and the little box with my wife's ring and necklace'. Regarding wine glasses, in the seventeenth century their delicacy was integral to their status since glass was a luxury, and their fragility means that such minimal survival is unsurprising.

▲ *Selection of animal bones found at the Gloucester wreck site.*

Each object, however fragmentary or everyday, can contribute to our knowledge of contemporary life in Restoration Britain. Thirteen animal bones have been found so far: eleven cow bones, and one each from a pig and a sheep. These finds back up what we know of seventeenth-century eating habits and navy victualling. Salted beef and pork, preserved in barrels, were staples of a seaman's diet. Mutton was not part of standard navy rations and sheep were likely carried live on board to provide fresh meat for the officers and highest status passengers – in this case the Duke of York and his courtiers. This sheep's bone might have been gnawed by the future King of England and Scotland himself!

Inevitably, our available information is partial. No muster list for those on board survives, so the total number of people drowned, as well as the names of some of the crew and passengers, remain anonymous. Ongoing research is filling in these gaps by searching archives for the wills of those who died, for instance, or by finding the names of survivors in muster lists of other navy ships who were recorded as transferring from the *Gloucester*. Unsurprisingly, the names of individuals of a higher social class, whether they drowned or survived, dominate in surviving records. Sometimes this information is also tantalisingly sparse. A newspaper article entitled 'A Letter from Scotland', which was clearly based on eyewitness testimonials, reported the death of 'an English Lady, whose name we cannot as yet learn'. The identity of this noblewoman still remains unknown: whether she was a wife, daughter, or sister to those on board, or perhaps a mistress, is likewise undetermined; but the inclusion of such a gossipy snippet was perhaps intended to draw attention to the pleasure-seeking intentions of James and his circle, and to the duke's reputation as a libertine.

Gathering evidence and information about those of humbler status is even more challenging. Our long-term aim is to piece together knowledge about all classes, nationalities, and races of people, and about women on board, creating as true a picture of the diverse range of the *Gloucester*'s passengers and crew as possible. ◼

Casualties of the *Gloucester* Tragedy

Between 130 and 250 people are thought to have died in the wreck of the *Gloucester* on 6 May 1682, though the exact number will probably never be known. Amongst the passengers who drowned were a group of Scottish noblemen and gentlemen including Robert Ker, 3rd Earl of Roxburghe; Sir John Hope, Laird of Hopetoun; Sir Joseph Douglas of Pumpherston; and Patrick Gordon of Nethermuir. The Irish nobleman Donogh O'Brian, Lord Ibrackan was just eighteen or nineteen when he drowned, whereas Hope was in his early thirties, and left behind his wife Margaret, daughter Helen, and his son and heir Charles, born the previous year.

▲ *Sir John Hope of Hopetoun, Jacobus Schuneman, c.1680. Hopetoun House collection.*

The Duke of York and the other elite passengers were joined on board by a large retinue of servants, many of whom drowned. Anthony Antwine, who had served in James' household since 1679 as his cook, Mr Holis, the duke's equerry, and Mr Shelton, the king's page, were all reported to have perished. But the royal household was not the only one affected. James Livingstone, a physician and servant of Sir David Falconer, President of the Session in Scotland, drowned, as did the servants of Patrick Gordon and the Earl of Roxburghe.

'our solace must be that the Duke is well arrived here, though with a greater loss in his train than we can yet make any just computation of'.
Samuel Pepys to William Hewer, Edinburgh, 8 May 1682.

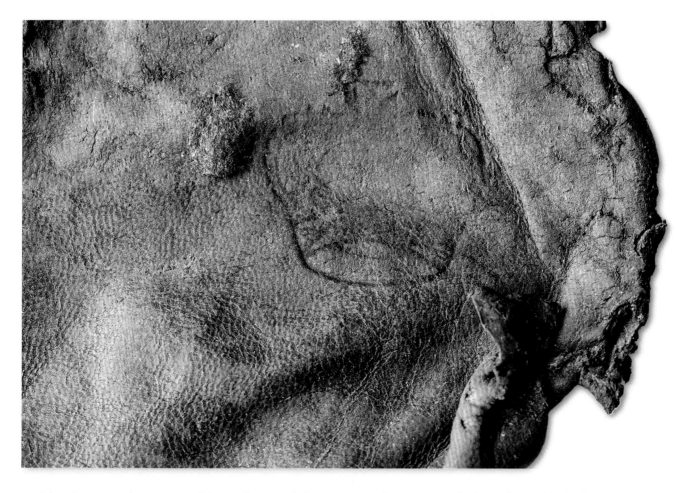

▲ *A leather pouch recovered from the wreck bears several crown symbols and was likely the property of one of James, Duke of York's servants.*

The largest group of victims came from the ship's crew, who were some of the last to attempt an escape from the sinking ship by jumping into the choppy waters of the North Sea. Many sailors were poor swimmers and drowned. The dependents of sixty-three of the *Gloucester*'s deceased crew received a bounty payment in compensation but the number who died is likely to have been much higher if the seamen without dependents are included. James Hyde, the 2nd lieutenant of the *Gloucester* drowned. Hyde was the youngest brother of Henry Hyde, 2nd Earl of Clarendon and Anne Hyde, the first wife of James, Duke of York. Peter Gardner, a midshipman, Robert Street, a quartermaster, and the ship's cook Francis Cranwell all drowned. The seriousness of the event is reflected in the number of widows and orphans created. The death of Robert Stowe left his wife Joanne and four children alone, while Mary and Elizabeth Goodwin were made orphans by the death of their father Thomas and money was given to the minister and churchwardens of Fareham in Hampshire for their support.

The tragedy also resulted in animal casualties since the duke is reported to have been travelling with his dogs. According to a satirical poem printed in 1704, James' royal hound Mumper drowned when, following a standoff, the dog lost possession of a floating wooden plank to the royal physician Sir Charles Scarburgh (see page 78), who barely survived the ordeal. ■

Musicians of the Serjeant-Trumpeter

James, Duke of York and his party were accompanied by a group of accomplished musicians to perform on board and at ceremonial events. Four royal trumpeters and a kettledrummer sailed on the *Gloucester*, playing for the royal party enroute but were also expected to perform as part of the royal progress into Edinburgh after disembarking at Leith. At the time, trumpets and kettledrums were not perceived as instruments for private entertainment but instead were designed principally for military troops and processions. To reflect this, a Serjeant-Trumpeter was appointed to manage the king's trumpeters and kettledrummers. In 1682, the holder of this office was Gervais Price, who was not on the 1682 voyage but would have been responsible for assigning the five individuals who were.

Walter Vanbright was the kettledrummer on board the *Gloucester* and had served the crown since about 1666, when he attended at sea on Prince Rupert of the Rhine, the cousin of Charles II and the Duke of York. Vanbright was in his late fifties in 1682 and drowned in the wreck. On 5 June 1682, £12 was paid to Gervais Price for a new pair of kettledrums to replace those lost at sea. Vanbright's widow Elizabeth was granted an annual pension by James after he became king. The Duke of York was clearly fond of kettledrums, and this led to their increased employment in royal service. At the Restoration of Charles II in 1660 only the Royal Guards were assigned kettledrums, after the accession of James II every regiment of horse was provided with them.

▲ *Order of procession for the coronation of James II (1685). © British Library Board. All Rights Reserved/ Bridgeman Images.*

The four royal trumpeters who travelled on the *Gloucester* were brothers Mathias and William Shore, Thomas Barwell, and John Stephens. Mathias Shore had only recently been appointed as trumpeter-in-ordinary in January 1682, whereas his brother had been sworn into the role three years earlier. Both survived the wreck, but it was Mathias who was especially proficient. He was one of eight trumpeters who marched in the coronation procession of James II on 23 April 1685 and in October 1687, he replaced Gervais Price as Serjeant-Trumpeter. The trumpeters performed on silver trumpets that were lost at sea. In 2008, a brass mouthpiece from a trumpet was rescued from the seabed. As mouthpieces were retractable and spares may have been needed, it is possible that a brass mouthpiece would have been attached to these silver instruments. Another possibility is that an additional trumpeter was on board belonging to the ship's company since naval vessels often had such a petty officer role. If the mouthpiece was part of a ship's instrument it would been made of brass, not silver.

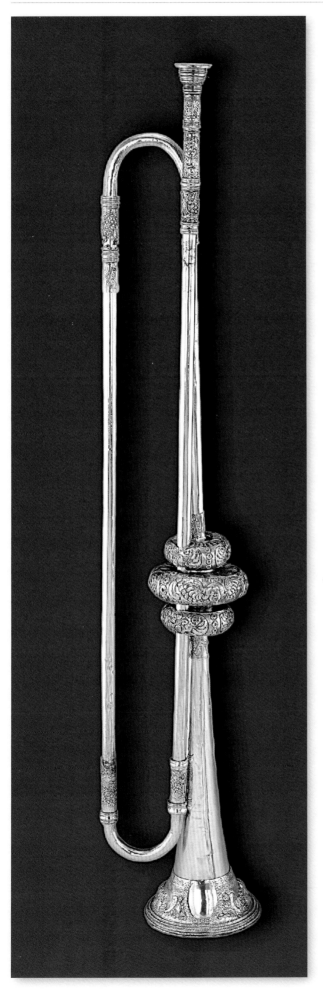

▼ *Brass trumpet mouthpiece recovered from the Gloucester wreck.*

◄ *Moncur trumpet, silver with brass mouthpiece, one of the few surviving trumpets comparable to those on the Gloucester. Reproduced with permission of the Mount Stuart Trust. Photography National Museums Scotland.*

Thomas Greeting and the king's private musick

A second group of royal musicians accompanied the Duke of York to Edinburgh. This group were part of the king's private musick which accompanied the royal court wherever it went and provided entertainment to the duke and his courtiers during their voyage. Ambient music would have been performed while they were dining on board and to amuse the travelling court as the ship sailed north. The private musick consisted of four divisions: wind instruments, lutes, violins, and voices, and though we don't know exactly what sort of performances were given on the *Gloucester*'s final voyage, we do know the identity of several of the musicians and the instruments they played. Thomas Farmer and Jeoffrey Aylesworth were violinists and were fortunate to survive the wreck. James Paisible, an oboe player originally from France also survived, as did Edmund (or Edward) Flower, who played both violin and theorbo, a type of lute. Joseph Fashion Snr, another violinist, is also believed to have been present, and was later recorded as having 'drowned at sea'.

The playing of music would have added to the jovial atmosphere on board as the Duke of York's return to political favour was celebrated. Although the *Gloucester* was cramped with so many passengers on board, music would have encouraged dancing, drinking, singing, and toasting to the Duke's permanent return to England.

Thomas Greeting, also a violinist of the king's private musick, drowned on the voyage. Greeting was a well-respected royal musician, having first been recorded as performing for Charles II's royal court in 1662 and on several prestigious occasions. He is most famous for his association with the flageolet, a wind instrument similar to the recorder but with a higher pitch. Greeting became a renowned teacher of this instrument and in 1668 he published *The Pleasant Companion, or New Lessons and Instructions for the Flageolet* which was later reprinted several times. Subsequent editions featured an image of him performing on the instrument.

▲ *Thomas Greeting's book, The Pleasant Companion, London, 1682,*
showing the frontispiece and one of the tunes on the facing page.
© British Library.

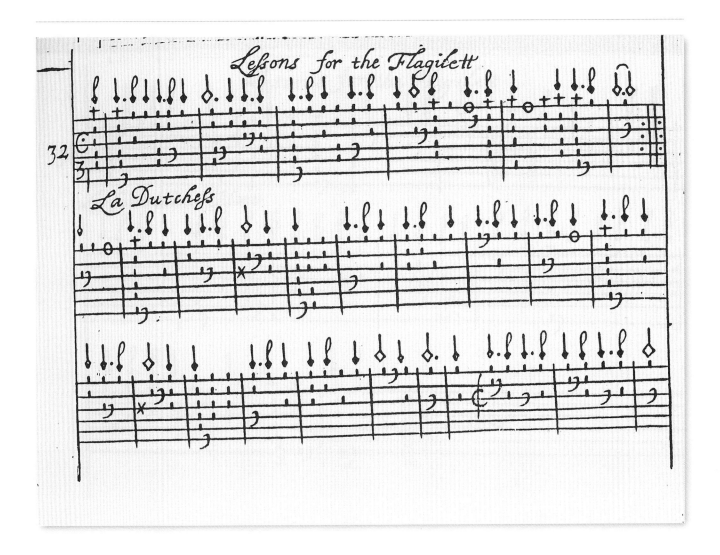

The publication of *The Pleasant Companion* assisted Greeting in becoming a distinguished teacher. The diarist and naval administrator Samuel Pepys recorded on several occasions in his diary how Greeting, 'the flageolet-master', had conducted lessons for both Pepys and his wife, Elisabeth. ■

One of the most intriguing assemblages of artefacts rescued from the wreck site concerns medicine and health. Attending the Duke of York on the *Gloucester* as his personal physician was Sir Charles Scarburgh (1615-94) and there was also a ship's surgeon on board, John Jones (died 1682), who was part of the crew. Scarburgh had been a royal physician since the 1660s and was travelling north to attend on the duke's pregnant wife Mary of Modena. Scarburgh's experiences on the *Gloucester* are particularly vivid and well documented. He did not evacuate with the Duke of York and had to jump into the sea as the ship sank, only surviving the ordeal by clinging to a plank of wood until he was picked up by the *Katherine* yacht's rowboat 'almost dead' according to Samuel Pepys. Scarburgh was sixty-seven at the time of the wreck. Stories about Scarburgh's miraculous survival were swiftly satirised since he was described as having to compete for the plank with one of James' dogs called Mumper.

▲ *Sir Charles Scarburgh, aged thirty-five, dressed in the red gown, hood, and cap of a Doctor of Physic, delivering an anatomy lesson, with Edward Arris, Master of the Worshipful Company of Barbers, Richard Greenbury, 1651. The Worshipful Company of Barbers.*

◀ *Urine flask rescued from the wreck site.*

A standout item, found on 6 July 2018 in the middle of the wreck site, is a distinctively shaped glass vessel. Clearly a urine flask, this was an essential item in every physician's equipment since urine was used to assess the health of a patient. This vessel could have been used daily to examine the Duke of York's urine. Other items also suggest medical use. These include a pewter porringer most likely employed as a bleeding bowl since bloodletting remained a widespread practice used to treat almost every condition, as it was believed to rid the body of impure fluids. The porringer rescued on 29 May 2012 from the middle of the wreck site includes on its handle or 'ear' a coat of arms, now indecipherable but indicating it to be a high-status item.

◀ *Pewter porringer, with its now indecipherable identifying coat of arms on the handle.*

The Royal Physician and the Medical Artefacts on the Gloucester

Two small apothecary glass bottles found together on the seabed may also have originally been part of a physician's medical equipment. It is possible that these items belonged to Scarburgh or were used by him.

▲ *Apothecary glass bottles found at the Gloucester wreck site.*

◄ *Another utensil with a medical use: a lidded jar probably made from lignum vitae wood containing a mustard-based substance almost certainly medicinal. This was found in Chest A (see page 63).*

We are able to recount Scarburgh's story in detail – researching historical documents and material objects that may relate to him, linking them to his portraits – due to his elite status. For many other passengers and crew, because of their class, it is not possible to do this. ∎

Afterword: The Future of the *Gloucester*: What happens next?

◀ *General Lord Richard Dannatt, Chair of the 1682 Trust, established to protect the Gloucester wreck site. Reproduced with permission of the University of East Anglia.*

The finding of the *Gloucester* is an internationally significant event. The project aims to conserve and display the *Gloucester*'s unique collection of artefacts and to share knowledge about the ship's remarkable history with this and future generations. It has the potential to revolutionise our understanding of the seventeenth century and of Norfolk's place in the world.

The generous support of the Leverhulme Trust is enabling historians at the University of East Anglia to research the life and times of the only surviving third-rate Cromwellian warship. They are writing a biography about its full career from inception to salvage across the seventeenth century, uncovering the *Gloucester*'s unique significance to national and international history.

As the exhibition 'The Last Voyage of the *Gloucester*: Norfolk's Royal Shipwreck, 1682' and this accompanying catalogue reveal, there remain numerous important research questions still to answer. These will require the input and collaboration of experts from a range of disciplines. Chemical analysis may tell us more about the origin of the wines and the varieties of grape used to make them as well as provide opportunities to create seventeenth-century style wine, a beverage relatively low in alcohol. Such a project could have significant commercial value as high alcohol drinks can have detrimental effects on society, and on health and wellbeing. New, lower alcohol wines with heritage appeal may make an attractive alternative. Considering the climate catastrophe that the world currently faces, the ullage captured in the sealed wine bottles provides unique opportunities for future research. Environmental and climate scientists may have much to learn from analysing the chemical markers of air from before the Industrial Revolution. Similarly, the composition and purpose of the compound in the *lignum vitae* jar, which includes mustard seeds, offers the potential to cultivate historic varieties of plants.

The Barnwell brothers and James Little, and the many experts who have contributed to the planning and management of the project, as well as the patrons who have supported its development, aim to raise awareness of the *Gloucester* and its importance through setting up a dedicated charity. I am privileged to be Chair of the 1682 Trust. With distinguished boards of advisors and experts in all relevant fields, the 1682 Trust seeks to protect the *Gloucester* and secure its heritage future by fundraising to develop a permanent home in Great Yarmouth to display artefacts from the wreck and train future maritime conservators and archaeological divers. The *Gloucester* could indeed become Norfolk's *Mary Rose*. ∎

Find out more

- The *Gloucester* Project website: https://www.gloucestershipwreck.co.uk

- Claire Jowitt, 'The Last Voyage of the *Gloucester* (1682): The Politics of a Royal Shipwreck', *The English Historical Review*, Volume 137, Issue 586, June 2022, Pages 728–762, https://doi.org/10.1093/ehr/ceac127

- Andrew Ashbee, David Lasocki, Peter Holman, and Fiona Kisby, *A Biographical Dictionary of English Court Musicians, 1485–1714*, 2 vols (Aldershot, 1998).

- David Burton, *Antique Sealed Bottles 1640-1900 and the Families that Owned Them*, 3 vols (ACC Publishing Group, 2015).

- Remmelt Daalder, *Van de Velde & Son, Marine Painters: The Firm of Willem van de Velde the Elder and Willem van der Velde the Younger, 1640-1707* (Primavera Pers, 2020).

- J. David Davies, *Kings of the Sea: Charles II, James II and the Royal Navy* (Seaforth Publishing, 2017).

- Richard Endsor, *The Master Shipwright's Secrets: How Charles II built the Restoration Navy* (Osprey Publishing, 2020).

- William A. Pettigrew, *Freedoms Debt: The Royal African Company and the Politics of the Atlantic Slave Trade, 1672-1752* (University of North Carolina Press, 2016).

Further Finds from the *Gloucester*

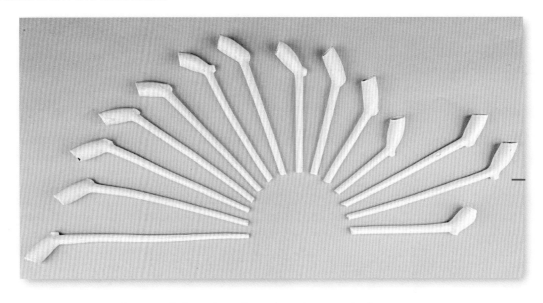

▲ *Group of clay pipes found at the wreck site.*

▲ *Set of three thimbles from Chest A.*

▲ *High quality knife handle of millefiori glass encasing an iron core found in Chest A.*